CW00656312

Loose Birds & game

Good Luck! Good Game!

All the best.

Andrew N. Ferm.

Also by Andrew Pern, Black Pudding and Foie Gras.

First published in 2010 in Great Britain by Face.
www.facepublications.com

A catalogue record of this book is available from the British Library.

ISBN 978-0-9558930-1-8

Art Direction & Design/Anthony Hodgson **www.weareface.com**

Photography/Drew Gardner **www.drewgardner.co.uk**
Additional photography/Marie Absolom and Lucinda Marland

Michel Roux photograph on page 10_11/reproduced with the kind permission of **Myburgh du Plessis**

British Gulls on page 294_295/reproduced with the kind permission of Tony Ladd **www.tonyladd.co.uk**

Loose Birds & Game Illustration on page 362/Tim Bulmer **www.timbulmerartist.com**

www.loosebirdsandgame.co.uk

Loose Birds & game

ANDREW PERN

FOREWORD/MICHEL ROUX

INTRODUCTION/BRIAN TURNER

WINE TASTING NOTES/ANDREW FIRTH

To mum & dad for rearing me into what I am today (I've got to blame somebody!), and to all of those country-types who live and work in our beautiful part of the world, 'God's own country'.

CONTENTS

10_11

Andrew with Michel Roux and Jean-Luc Naret, Director-general of Michelin, on 18th May 2010 at The Waterside Inn, Bray, which Michel co-owns with his son, Alain. Celebrating the 25th anniversary of The Waterside Inn being awarded its third Michelin Star.

FOREWORD
/MICHEL ROUX

The foodies in and around North Yorkshire are extremely lucky to have a chef in their neck of the woods who loves his surroundings, the people, the location and the local produce. Andrew has a 'wicked' personality which makes him lovable and inspires the young chefs around him.

I love Andrew's first book, but this one is so close to my heart. I adore game...all of it. I await the shooting season with anticipation and my palate waters for the variety of flavours, from mild to intense.

Being a shot, nothing can be more fulfilling than to shoot, prepare, cook and eat one's bag. Andrew's simple approach will attract people from all walks of life, who will be thrilled with the sophisticated results. Game is healthy, low in cholesterol and cheap. We should all be eating more of it. This is a book to use, and a copy belongs in every kitchen. As a matter of fact, it has already triggered a few ideas of my own....

Brian Turner, one of Andrew's fellow
Yorkshiremen, is one of Britain's most
successful and respected celebrity chefs.
He's managed to combine running many
highly respected restaurants in the UK
with a high-profile TV career.

INTRO

14_15

Who would have thought that the shy young man from Scarborough Tech could become one of Yorkshire's finest in such a short space of time? Well, I did - honest. Back in those early days when I did the 'Mallyan Spout Gourmet Weekend', Andrew and others came to give us a hand, and it was obvious then that he was going to make it.

Andrew's attitude, as well as skill, showed he was a worker and a perfectionist, and, if you look at his figure today, a bit like mine, you can see that he loves his food! My memories of those days, and today as well, are all happy ones and all based on driving over those wonderful North Yorkshire Moors (most people have no idea how beautiful they are) and then into Whitby for fish and chips at The Magpie, along with a bottle of Dom Perignon, and then outside for a big fat cigar.

Andrew has made his reputation in Harome and is now known worldwide, Michelin-starred and loved by many, with a Sunday lunch which is one of the best there is, as far as I am concerned. The other reason that many people visit the area is to enjoy the legendary shooting parties. Game in this part of the world is in great supply and of such a fantastic quality that, together with Andrews' expert cooking, makes a dream partnership.

DUCTION

SO WHAT ABOUT THE TITLE 'LOOSE BIRDS AND GAME'?
WELL, CHEFS [AND I SPEAK FOR MANY, BUT NOT ALL]
LIKE TO LIVE THE HIGH LIFE. WE DO WORK HARD, BUT, BOY
CAN WE PLAY HARD, AND THERE IS NO DOUBT THAT LOOSE
BIRDS AND GAME ARE SOMETHING MANY DREAM ABOUT.
WHEN YOU'VE FOUND YOUR LOOSE BIRD OR GAME,
THIS BOOK WILL TELL EVERYONE WHAT TO DO WITH IT,
HOW TO TREAT IT — AND ENJOY THE FOOD!

/BRIAN TURNER CBE

The sight of Roe Deer, Pheasants and Partridge feeding together on a crisp carpet of virgin snow beside our pond at Bank House, illuminated by an enormous floodlight was like a scene from a West End show, 'The theatre of the countryside', instantly grabbed my imagination as a child and has stayed with me ever since. At that moment, my love affair with 'Loose Birds and Game' began.

LOOSE BI
& GAME

/ANDREW PERN

RDS

Loose Birds & Game delivers a fresh approach to the often dark and dismal autumnal and winter dishes normally associated with 'game'. Ruddy cheeks and red noses are replaced with the virtues of low traceable fat in venison, the rarity of being able to eat grouse as a stew, salads that will be the envy of every Knightsbridge restaurant, with ladies that lunch, to snacks that the kids will devour and, to keep everyone happy, there's even a tipple for Granddad. I've always wanted to showcase the heritage and versatility of game as part of what defines my idea of 'British-ness', but in a light and informative mood. I want to make some of the foods that make Britain great, more accessible and appealing to a larger and more interested audience. It's amazing how easy it is to find local game and even some loose birds, if you are prepared to look in the right places – try your local butchers, farmers' markets, good neighbourhood supermarkets or the 'ye olde country-type shoppe' and take advantage of searching online. It's like anything in life, if you don't ask, you don't get!

'Salade Pérnigourdine'

Our version of the famous French 'Périgourdine' [the term used for dishes incorporating truffle] which is known by certain luminaries in Yorkshire, 'the food capital of Europe', as 'Pérnigourdine'.

WHY 'LOOSE BIRDS AND GAME'? A QUESTION I'VE ASKED MYSELF ON MORE THAN ONE OCCASION. IN FACT, QUITE FREQUENTLY. ACTUALLY, MOST DAYS!

I like to think that my take on life in general is fairly light-hearted and easy-going (although vast numbers of Commis Chefs would possibly challenge this, maybe?) and I hope that comes across in this book about our lives, surrounded by the breathtakingly beautiful and plentiful North Yorkshire Moors, the alpinesque woodlands and the 'uphill, downdale' countryside, where I've been lucky enough to be born and bred. I tend to take it all in my stride and consider it to be the norm, but to others, I guess it must seem foreign in many ways.

The variety of game and quality produce we have right on our doorstep is incredible, so it's no coincidence that we ended up at The Star. We chose the location for that exact reason. It provides the perfect backdrop for Nature's greatest larder to supply one of the county's most loved and celebrated Inns.

The Star has always had, and hopefully always will have, a true sense of being, honesty and unique qualities, which I trust extend into this book. We're a part of the countryside and The Star itself belongs to the country-folk. We play a vital role on the landscape of these often-strange 'PC' times. To a certain extent, rules are there to be broken in these parts, and you'll find that common sense comes built-in.

The simplicity of some of my dishes, the no-nonsense preparation and execution is what I want to share throughout the book. It contains a mixture of homely dishes, snacks, and even the odd tipple, through to the slightly more complex, restaurant dishes if you like - the difference between us and them!

20_21

CHEEP! CHEEP! CHEEP! THE FIRST MEMORY OF GAME I RECOLLECT — PHEASANT CHICKS.

I'd walk the 100 or so yards along the back road every day, my legs brushing against soaking wet dock leaves, a bucket of meal in one hand, and a stick to bash aside the damp foliage in the other. Climbing the rocky stone steps of the old granary, I'd be halfway up, and then I'd get the smell of warm sawdust shavings and the faint noise of the cheeping chicks inside. When I reached the top, the chink of the latch of the rickety old door clicked, then the noise levels seemed to heighten to what seemed like an almost deafening pitch, to a five year old boy.

As I half lifted, half scraped the door open, the shafts of light seemed to shine down from above, almost heavenly, onto the plywood circle of life. Lit and warmed by a 60 watt bulb, the baby birds clambered and somersaulted over each other. As each mealtime came and went, day after day, week after week, the makeshift incubator grew in width, as the birds grew in size, and the 'Charlie Tunner Band' was slackened to give more breathing space to the birds that were soon to become fair game.

The word 'Game' always brings all manner of memories flooding back to me - my senses as a child were filled with a whole range of sights, sounds and scents of the countryside. The perfect, still summer days of the purple-clad North Yorkshire Moors above Rosedale Abbey, where I used to work in times gone by. The honeyed perfume of coarse heather, with its deep crimson and purple hues... remind me of a place 'Grandpop' would take refuge after he was diagnosed with a serious illness. All the nice things in his life were banned, but he seemed fairly content. No wonder, as one day travelling back home, we found him pulled over by a grouse butt on Simon Foster's Egton Estate with a 'Ford's' Pork Pie and half a bottle of whisky! We thought he was taking his illness well, but what better place for a bit of bait and a nip of whisky, than on top of the world in the middle of August surrounded by coveys of grouse whistling overhead. Contentment indeed... I always knew pork pies had healing qualities!

24_25

FAST FORWARD TWENTY FIVE YEARS…
AND THEN YOU HAVE THE CHEF'S SIDE OF IT.

...LOOSE BIRDS AND GAME! IT MAY, OR MAY NOT,
EVOKE SOME SORT OF REACTION DEPENDING ON YOU
AS AN INDIVIDUAL. IT MAY EVEN RAISE THE ODD EYEBROW!

I'm now invited by American businessmen, bigwigs and regulars alike, at least twice every week onto the fine estates which surround us in Ryedale. Some may be syndicate days, some, rough shoots from the village, or indeed, the 'proper job' days of Duncombe Park Estate in Helmsley, owned by Lord and Lady Feversham. It is, of course, great to be asked but, and it is quite a big but, who cooks and looks after them on their return? As much as I'd like to take them all up on their kind offers, The Star is the heartbeat of all of this hospitality and it has to be right all of the time, or it would start to dilute everything that we've worked for over the last fourteen or so years. I'm sure in years to come, I'll be able to delegate and relax. It would be nice to see the full cycle again, from the day-old chicks to the splendour of the day's shoot.

Anybody who knows of me (really the vast numbers of people in the catering trade, especially the lovable rogues known as chefs), will know of my 'work hard, play hard' attitude, which is a label that our hectic profession has been tagged with over the years (probably for good reason). Our notoriety might have something to do with our long unsociable hours, working away from home, being surrounded by good-looking front of house girls and constantly blossoming new relationships, which all lead to the well-publicised 'caged animal antics' you read about. There aren't many quiet, shy and retiring types in our trade. If you add a drop of the old charm, you would be surprised how much trouble chefs get themselves into!

Chefs have recently become almost like 'superstars', with celebrity status, and cooking is the new 'Rock and Roll'! There is (fortunately!) great interest surrounding food and dining out nowadays, and everyone wants to know who's behind the scenes and who's at the stove, playing the 'old piano' (to borrow a term from the French). This inevitably puts the spotlight directly onto chefs, which in turn attracts the attention of attractive girls and, dare I say it, bored housewives, wanting to get to know how to do things our way. How game? is one thing. How loose? is not for the faint-hearted!

I hope you enjoy
my take on life
and food in the
countryside, as
much as I enjoy
doing my bit, and
being part of such
a beautiful corner
of the world.
I assure you, life
is never much of
a hardship here!

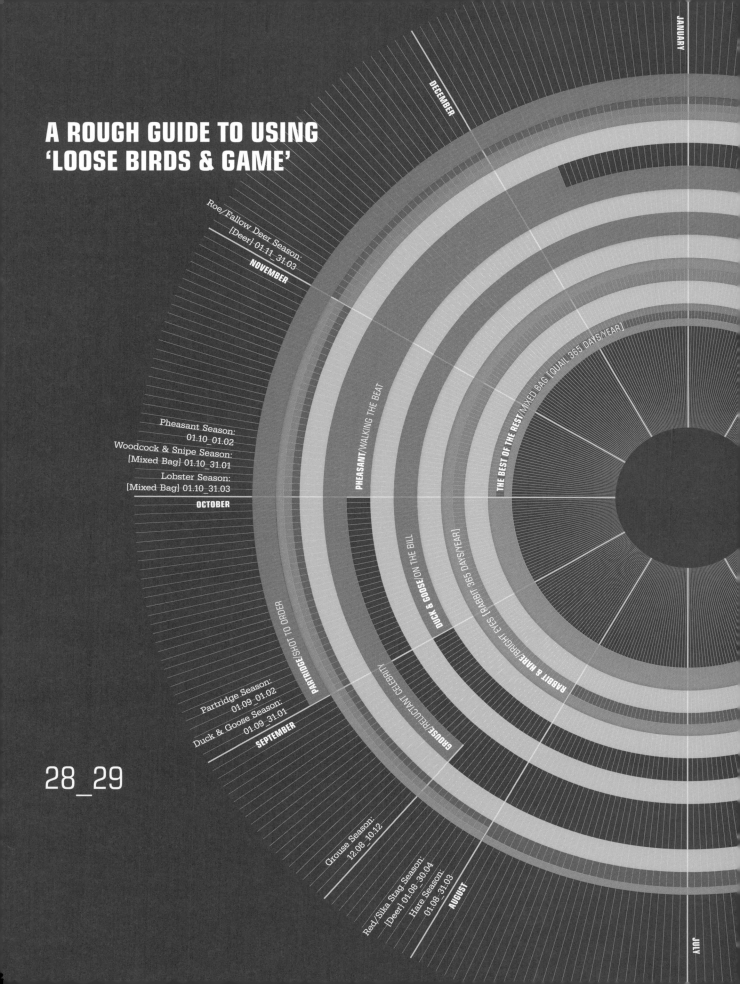

A ROUGH GUIDE TO USING 'LOOSE BIRDS & GAME'

28_29

Roe/Fallow Deer Season:
[Deer] 01.11_31.03
NOVEMBER

Pheasant Season:
01.10_01.02
Woodcock & Snipe Season:
[Mixed Bag] 01.10_31.01
Lobster Season:
[Mixed Bag] 01.10_31.03
OCTOBER

Partridge Season:
01.09_01.02
Duck & Goose Season:
01.09_31.01
SEPTEMBER

Grouse Season:
12.08_10.12

Red/Sika Stag Season:
[Deer] 01.08_30.04
Hare Season:
01.08_31.03
AUGUST

DECEMBER

JANUARY

JULY

PHEASANT/WALKING THE BEAT

PARTRIDGE/SHOT TO ORDER

GROUSE/RELUCTANT CELEBRITY

DUCK & GOOSE/ON THE BILL

RABBIT & HARE/BRIGHT EYES [RABBIT 365 DAYS/YEAR]

THE BEST OF THE REST/MIXED BAG [QUAIL 365 DAYS/YEAR]

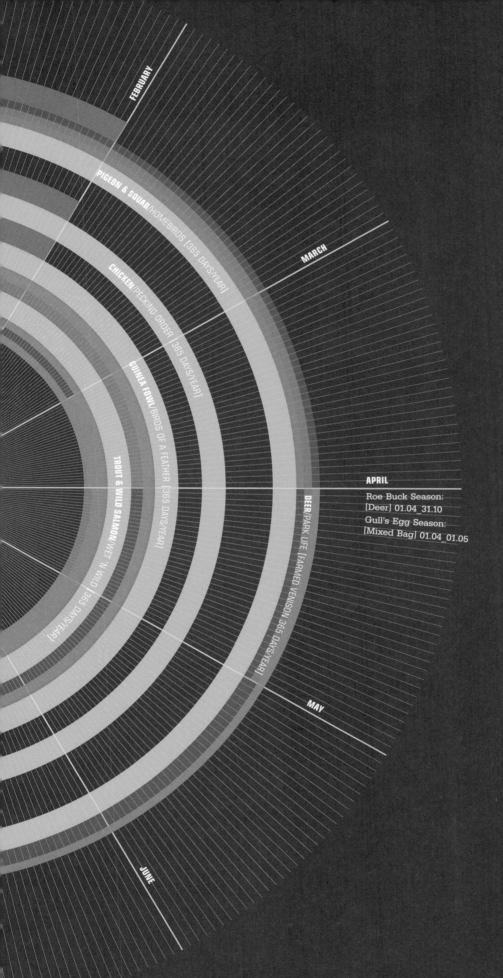

Within the circular diagram:

FEBRUARY

PIGEON & SQUAB/HOMEBIRDS [365 DAYS/YEAR]

CHICKEN/PECKING ORDER [365 DAYS/YEAR]

GUINEA FOWL/BIRDS OF A FEATHER [365 DAYS/YEAR]

TROUT & WILD SALMON/WET 'N' WILD [365 DAYS/YEAR]

DEER/PARK LIFE [FARMED VENISON 365 DAYS/YEAR]

MARCH

APRIL
Roe Buck Season:
[Deer] 01.04_31.10
Gull's Egg Season:
[Mixed Bag] 01.04_01.05

MAY

JUNE

This guide is based around life in North Yorkshire. Availability will vary depending on your location.

GAME SEASON/AUGUST

GROUSE: The One and Only legendary first-of-the-season game bird, peerless in every way; its individual diet giving an individual taste. The Glorious Twelfth marks the start of the Game Calendar.

HARE: There is an intense flavour to this dark-meated creature, capable of land speeds of 40mph. The huge numbers in farmland surrounding The Star allows us to use up this delicious meat in a great variety of ways.

GAME SEASON/SEPTEMBER

PARTRIDGE: 'French' Red-legged or 'English' Grey-legged, farmed or wild; whatever sort of leg man you are, all are delicious, although wild ones have the edge due to their foraged diet.

DUCK & GOOSE: Known as 'wildfowl', they are widely available especially mallard, which is shot mainly in coastal or marshland areas.

GAME SEASON/OCTOBER

PHEASANT: The quintessential game bird with their distinctive oriental plumage and splendour, are estate-managed and in abundance throughout the winter months. Young for the pan; old for the pot!

WOODCOCK & SNIPE: A true delicacy. Difficult to shoot, but delicious to eat! These elusive, long-beaked wetland waders have a pleasant, milder game flavour. They are much sought-after and can be expensive.

GAME SEASON/365 DAYS/YEAR

DEER: Venison, the generic name for all deer, is essentially wild and normally only shot on estates and moorland as part of a cull to curb numbers. It provides healthy, good eating with very little waste, and is gaining popularity with butchers and supermarkets. Farmed venison is also available all year round.

RABBIT: One of the cheapest wild foods available, although not as popular as it should be; its tender, pale pink, tasty meat deserving a much wider appeal.

SUPPLIERS

THESE SUPPLIERS ARE MOSTLY SPECIALISTS THAT I'VE USED FOR MANY YEARS AT THE STAR. SOME SUPPLY HARD-TO-FIND SEASONAL PRODUCTS AND OTHERS SUPPLY GOODS ALL YEAR-ROUND. IN MY OPINION THEY ARE THE BEST SUPPLIERS I'VE USED, AND THE BEST IN THE BUSINESS. QUALITY AND CONSISTENCY IS THE RECIPE FOR MOST OF THEIR SUCCESS, AND THAT'LL DO FOR ME. I KNOW THEY'LL ALL LOOK AFTER YOU.

CHEESE

Lowna Dairy
Raywell, Near Cottingham,
East Yorkshire HU16 5YL
Phone +44 (0)1482 670 570
www.lownadairy.com
Lovely pasteurised produce from the rolling East Yorkshire Wolds; stable cheese, great for cooking, and consistently winning awards.

Neal's Yard Dairy
108 Druid Street,
London SE1 2HH
Phone +44 (0)20 7500 7654
www.nealsyarddairy.co.uk
Beautifully matured and treated cheeses from the British Isles used in a lot of our dishes.

Shepherds Purse Cheeses
Leachfield Grange, Newsham,
Thirsk, North Yorkshire YO7 4DJ
Phone +44 (0)1845 587 220
www.shepherdspurse.co.uk
We've used Bell family's cheese since day one, long before Star Inn times. Lovely cheeses, lovely people.

FISH & SHELLFISH

Hodgson's Fish
5 Whitby Street,
Hartlepool TS24 7AD
Phone +44 (0)1429 273 169
www.hodgsonfish.co.uk
I've known Alan for many years, he supplies us with sea trout, lobster and other superb produce from the North Sea. He's also a seasoned arm-wrestler!

Yoadwath Mill Trout Farm
Yoadwath Mill, Kirkbymoorside,
York YO62 7LS
Phone +44 (0)1751 433 002
We get lovely smoked local trout and air-dried ham from Andy Stewart, another long-standing supplier of ours.

FORAGED FOOD

Miles Irving
www.forager.org.uk

We have great days-out, and fantastic meals whenever foraging around Harome. There's a fascinating larder growing in and around the hedgerows, and foraging is excellent for sustainability!

The Mountain Food Company
www.mountainfood.org
Mountain Food is a top supplier of various foraged foods, and more unusual items from farther afield.

GAME SUPPLIES

Derek Fox
25 Market Place, Malton,
North Yorkshire YO17 7LP
Phone **+44 (0)1653 600 338**
www.derekfoxbutchers.co.uk
A lovely, old-fashioned butchers in the picturesque market town of Malton. Seeing the seasonal array of local game hanging in the shop-front is a real treat.

Lishman's of Ilkley
25 Leeds Road, Ilkley,
North Yorkshire LS29 8DP
Phone **+44 (0)1943 609 436**
www.lishmansonline.co.uk
Known for their exceptional quality, Lishman's supply to the finest shops in the country. It's an absolute mouth-watering pleasure to look around their shop, if you're ever in downtown Ilkley!

Yorkshire Game
Station Road Industrial Park,
Brompton on Swale, Richmond,
North Yorkshire DL10 7SN
Phone +44 (0)1748 810 212
www.yorkshiregame.co.uk
A great accessible source of game, with a diverse range available to order online.

GOURMET SUPPLIERS

Harrods Food Hall
87–135 Brompton Road,
Knightsbridge, London SW1X 7XL
Phone +44 (0)20 8479 5100
www.harrods.com

Gulls' eggs, game, truffles, wild
mushrooms, etc; this 'average' corner
shop(!), has something for everyone.

Teesdale Trencherman
Scargill Lodge, Barnard Castle,
County Durham DL12 9SY
Phone +44 (0)7854 613026
www.trencherman.co.uk

Most wild things are readily available,
as is a variety of other fine produce.

HAMPERS

The Star Inn Corner Shop
Harome, near Helmsley,
North Yorkshire YO62 5JE
Phone +44 (0)1439 770082
www.thestaratharome.co.uk

Various cheeses, wild mushrooms,
truffles, and a lot more on offer from
our little shop. We can supply every
ingredient in this book, when in season!

KITCHEN EQUIPMENT

Chef Superstore
Unit 5, Odeon Buildings,
Blossom Street, York YO24 1AJ
Phone +44 (0)1904 466 390
www.chefsuperstore.co.uk

Irish Tony has great products
and he's always 'ready to do a deal'.
Including supplying the Schönwald
porcelain and tableware for this book.

Continental Chef Supplies
7-8 Burdon Street, North West
Industrial Estate, Peterlee,
County Durham SR8 2JH
Phone 0800 988 8981
www.chefs.net

Paul Goodfellow supplies probably the
best kitchenware in the country.

Peter Maturi
84-86 Vicar Lane, Leeds LS1 7JH
Phone +44 (0)113 245 3887
www.maturionline.co.uk

Excellent for professional and amateur
chefs alike, based in the heart of Leeds;

MEAT SUPPLIES

R & J Catering Butchers
Wateredge, Longswales Lane,
Kirkby Malzeard, Ripon
North Yorkshire HG4 3RJ
Phone +44 (0)1765 658 611

Rob and Ryan, father and son, have
been supplying me for over twenty
years; it's always a pleasure to do
business with them.

Radford's Butchers
81 Coach Road, Sleights, Whitby,
North Yorkshire YO22 5EH
Phone +44 (0)1947 810 229

I've known Andrew Radford since I
was about eight years old. He supplies
us mainly with Aged York Hams;
he's one of the few suppliers of this
speciality in the UK.

POULTRY

Loose Birds and Game
Sunnyside, Harome,
Near Helmsley,
North Yorkshire YO62 5JF
Phone +44 (0)1439 770 683

Paul Talling, my local free range poultry
supplier, whose company gave me the
idea for the name of my book. He has
beautiful chickens, ducks and geese,
and is literally on our doorstep!

RARE BREED PORK

Taste Tradition
Units I & J, Lumley Close,
Thirsk Industrial Park, Thirsk,
North Yorkshire YO7 3TD
Phone +44 (0)1845 525 330
www.tastetradition.co.uk

Charles Ashbridge, together with
his mother, runs a brilliant catering
Butcher's, supplying country pubs
locally and businesses such as Harrods
and Fortnum and Mason, as well as
some of the top London restaurants.

SHOOTING PARTIES

Justin Birkett
Email mail@rievaulxsporting.com

Justin offers a mixed bag of pheasants
and partridges on his beautiful Rievaulx
shoot. Based near the haunting ruins of
the Abbey to the north of Helmsley.

VEGETABLES, FRUIT & GENERAL PROVISIONS

Fodder
Great Yorkshire Showground,
Harrogate HG2 8NZ
Phone +44 (0)1423 546 111
www.fodderweb.co.uk

A superstore of Yorkshire's greatest
produce, all under one roof.

Taylor's of Pickering
42 Market Place, Pickering,
North Yorkshire YO18 7AE
Phone +44 (0)1751 472 170
www.top.uk.com

When I was a child, Keith Taylor's
father used to smoke the salmon my
grandfather caught in the River Esk.
I've since bought that 'old smoker' to
do our curing at The Star, which stands
up well to our experimental ways!!

Richard Wellock & Sons
Whiteholme Mill, Skipton Road,
Trawden, Colne, Lancashire BB8 8RA
Phone +44 (0)8453 383 838
www.wellocks.com

Richard's son, James, has become one
of our main suppliers of, well, just about
everything! It was initially fruit and
vegetables, but James likes a challenge
and finds it hard to say no, if we require
any new products.

WINE MERCHANTS

Firth & Co. Wine Merchants
Newton Bank, Newton le Willows,
Bedale, North Yorkshire DL8 1TE
Phone +44 (0)1677 451 952
www.firthandco.com

My old mate, Firthy! We've been
through thick and thin. He's a great
friend and a proper supplier, who will
source any wine, but only of quality,
and he's always willing to open a bottle
to have a taste. Thank you for your witty
input with the Tasting Notes. Cheers!

WINE TASTING NOTES
/ANDREW FIRTH

After training as a wine merchant in London for 10 years, I moved back to my family's home in Yorkshire. I knew the area well, so ended up working for Yorkshire Fine Wines, covering the North Yorkshire 'patch', which included the beautiful Yorkshire Moors.

A good customer of mine, The Mallyan Spout Hotel, in Goathland, in the depths of 'Heartbeat' country, was owned by the Heslop family. I used to organise gourmet dinners at the hotel, where I'd discuss wine, and Brian Turner (pre-TV fame) would do the food bit. It was Peter Heslop, along with Bill Symonds (the actor and big foodie) who visited The Milburn Arms in Rosedale one day, and told me about the young couple there, and how good their food was. That was my first knowledge of Pernie...

Over the years, I've always attempted to teach Andrew more about wine and champagne, but I've always been impressed with Andrew's desire to 'keep it real' at The Star; his 'love' of beer drinking, and encouragement of country pub antics are always on the agenda. As he says himself, it's a pub first and foremost.

A couple of years ago, I organised a trip for several of Yorkshire's finest establishments to see Dom Perignon, Château de Saran - the Möet and Chandon Château - and Bollinger, visiting the vineyards and cellars of these world-famous wine houses. After the 'research' (a full day's wining and dining), my 'star' pupil needed a little relaxation, so we decided on a game of boules, in the grounds of the Möet Château. With the shutters and French windows wide open, Eugene McCoy tinkling the ivories, the setting was perfect - apart from the fact it was the early hours and pitch black! This wasn't a problem for Pernie, as he invented the aim-at-the-candle version of the game. The only problem was that the swoosh of the boule either blew out the candle or knocked it over – it was a very long game!

On another social occasion, Andrew and Jacquie invited me to join them on an 'away day' in London, at the prestigious Catey Awards. Always generous, hospitable, and very friendly with all of the top chefs, Andrew got into the swing of things easily as the hardier element of the catering industry relaxed in the Red Bar at The Grosvenor House Hotel on Park Lane – we never saw him again until 7am the next morning!

You'll notice a theme...

Not too long ago, The Star celebrated a decade of Pern ownership, so Chef and I decided to organise a 'Proper Lunch'. As the afternoon wore on, we became more boisterous as the wine flowed. At some point, Pernie and I decided to arm-wrestle; it seemed a suitable thing to do at that stage of the evening. He beat me with ease, and then went around the table playing winner-stays-on. Last up, was the reserved fishmonger from Hartlepool, Mr Hodgson, who quietly destroyed our champion on each of, probably, five attempts as our hero tried to come back. The fishmonger said little, claiming beginners' luck. One or two raised eyebrows later, Andrew gave in as graciously as only he can! The next morning, AP was back at work and the fishmonger's son, calling for the day's order, asked whether his father had behaved, or if he had been up to his party trick, after a few drinks? What was that, asked Andrew. Arm-wrestling! We had been hustled...

Our friendship and business relationship has gone from strength to strength over the years. Although he's 10 years younger than me, and beer drinking is still important, slowly, his love and knowledge of wine is growing. Pernie has a style of cooking that suits classical wines, so I look forward to tasting many more with him, over the next decade!

Andrew Firth, of Firth & Co.
Wine Merchant, bon vivant,
raconteur and a great mate.

MATCHING WINES WITH FOOD IS ALWAYS AN INTERESTING CHALLENGE AND, WHEN SUCCESSFUL, ADDS ENJOYMENT TO THE DISH AND THE MEAL IN GENERAL. THE SLIGHT FAULT WITH THE WHOLE PROCESS IS PEOPLE'S OWN PREFERENCES, SO THAT, IF SAUTERNES IS THE PERFECT MATCH TO FOIE GRAS, THEN MARVELLOUS, BUT, IF UNCLE TED DOESN'T PARTICULARLY LIKE SWEET WINES, THEN IT'S "NO RUDDY MATCH" FOR HIM. EQUALLY, IF AUNTIE LIL CAN'T DRINK RIOJA, THEN IT'S NO MATCH FOR THE SPECIAL LAMB DISH. PUTTING ALL OF THAT ASIDE, I HAVE MATCHED SOME WINES TO ANDREW'S CLASSIC DISHES — SOME IDEAS ARE SAFER THAN OTHERS! THROUGHOUT THE REMAINDER OF THE BOOK, YOU'LL FIND MY WINE NOTES AT THE BEGINNING OF EACH FOLD-OUT SECTION.

ME

PARTRIDGE: PLUMP, TASTY BREASTS AND A TRIM THIGH, WITH A LOVELY LIGHT FLAVOUR. A GREAT MIDDLE-OF-THE-ROAD BIRD FOR ALL NEWCOMERS TO GAME, OR NOVICE DINERS.

DRIVINGGA

The 'driven' days of the red-legged partridge are always popular around these parts, and Justin Birkett's Rievaulx shoot is rated one of the best in the country, which is quite possibly for the entertainment and hospitality, as well as the shooting, of course! Rievaulx drives, such as 'Charlie's', 'Henry's', 'George's', and the American sounding 'Critters', christened by the late Tom Tracy (of Tracy/Ford Motors fame), offer a varied bag of feathered pick 'n' mix: mallard, pigeon, crow, pheasant and partridge (amongst other critters!) can all be shot on one shoot. All in all, a feast of food falling from the skies.

The number of birds shot on a day's shoot varies, as venues offer a 200 or 300 (or more) bird day. They only take a brace or two for themselves, and the rest are sold onto their local game dealer, and then distributed in the food chain around the country, and across Europe.

Game is wonderfully healthy, low in fat and high in protein, inexpensive and easy to cook! It is, after all, some of the finest food that flies, runs or swims free in the wild. Fair game, indeed, but, in these politically correct and, to be honest, bloody boring times, the average supermarket shopper would rather buy a flaccid, insipid, battery chicken than a chubby grey-legged partridge, or a full-of-flavour cock pheasant. Hence, the majority of our game finds its way to the Continent, where the appreciation of good food, in general, is a way of life and part of society, rather than a matter of convenience and cost.

The loaders and drivers, all local lads, always have breakfast with 'Chef' on the breakfast bar in our shooting lodge, across the road from The Star. Bacon butties and pots of strong tea kick-start the day, as we await the arrival of our guests, who dine in the more formal surroundings of our private dining room, before being introduced to their 'Guns' for the day. The lads all tend to be country-types, who 'advise' our guests on where (or how) to stand, and in which direction to shoot etc. Practical fonts of all knowledge on all number of drives in the area, and on all manner of subjects.

Shot to Order

40_43

GREY-LEGGED, LOCAL SHOT PARTRIDGE WITH BRAISED GREEN LENTILS, CELERY AND BACON BUNDLES AND FINO SHERRY JUICES

44_47

RIEVAULX RED-LEGGED PARTRIDGE WITH A 'BEETROOT FONDANT', CUMBRIAN SPECK, BUTTERED BRUSSELS SPROUTS AND WALNUTS

48_49

RISOTTO OF RIEVAULX RED-LEGGED PARTRIDGE WITH PENNY BUN MUSHROOMS, WILTED 'MATADOR' GARDEN SPINACH AND DODDINGTON'S CHEESE AND THYME WAFER

50_53

SAGE-ROAST RIEVAULX RED-LEGGED PARTRIDGE WITH KILN-SMOKED YOADWATH MILL HAM, CREAMED CELERIAC, SLOE GIN JUICES AND BUTTERED BABY BEETS

54_57

GREY-LEGGED PARTRIDGE AND FOIE GRAS TERRINE, CRISP SKIN, VICTORIA PLUM JELLY AND SOURDOUGH CRISPS

Wine Notes - Partridge
by Andrew Firth

Young partridge are a lovely, light, fresh, clean meat and, therefore, the wine needs to reflect this. Early in the season, a cru Beaujolais would be good: Fleurie, Morgon or a fruity Brouilly. Later in the year, when the weather is colder, maybe the richer dishes would better suit the sweet, ripe fruit of the Rhône valley, such as Chateauneuf du Pape or Rioja Crianza or, into the New World, and you could go with a New Zealand Pinot Noir. The Risotto, being different, would be good with a Pinot Gris from New Zealand, a fruity white wine with a slightly spicy character, but don't serve it too cold!

Clouds of partridges - the driven birds, started spiralling out of control overhead. We were now on Badger Corner, the steep incline divided by the rather out-of-place electricity pylons that divide the woodland. The freezing fog started to roll in, and as the temperature dropped, so did morale. I think that the previous night's entertainment might have had something to do with that, as the amount of alcohol in our systems was currently neck-and-neck with the amount of blood!

In between drives, there was, as there always is, a lot of banter. One of the day's guns, Richard Kelvin-Hughes, was clad in just a shirt and a waistcoat fleece. We couldn't understand why he wasn't feeling the bitter cold like everybody else that day. 'Viking blood!', he explained, as he threw Jacquie over his shoulder whilst teetering on the edge of the lake, looking like a 'dead-cert' for an early dip as he pirouetted out of control. He couldn't work out if it was one of Jacquie's nipples poking into his back, or one of the buttons from her shooting coat – it really was that cold! I took advantage of the day's events, and had freshly shot birds in each overcoat pocket, acting as feathered hand-warmers. I don't think they'll ever catch on in the High Street!

Guns at the ready, we waited for Justin to blow the whistle again. Maybe it was just psychological, but as we waited, spread out around the semi-frozen lake, it seemed like an eternity for the second drive to eventually begin. This time, as the whistle still reverberated in my ears, they flew towards us from the corner of Spring Lake.

As the pheasants, partridges, and the odd crow fell from the sky, the flurry of lead-shot followed, sprinkling the lakes like an autumn shower. Bundles of feathered creatures bounced through the trees like a giant pinball machine. The dogs scattered in every direction to collect the haul, like a well-oiled machine, scurrying through the undergrowth, into the water and along the hedgerows, picking up the birds with gusto and precision. Each of the dogs returned, time after time, clenching a bird firmly and delicately between their jaws.

As with all shooting days, the day was punctuated with the odd glass of champagne or an occasional nip of sloe gin with a slice of pie. A well needed little piece of sustenance when shooting 'through', if there's no break for lunch.

After the shoot, we returned to The Star, the convoy of Range Rovers entered the village, our burning chiminea greeted us at the entrance to the pub – it's the simplest of things and gives a warm welcome, as the stack of logs alongside gently dwindles – many of the guests like to throw a token piece of wood into the flames, like some kind of peace-offering. Behind the chiminea, on the trellis fencing, hung wild duck and red-legged partridge, tied up in a row like an execution line. The warmth of the fire fights against the billowing piles of leaves from the old sycamore tree opposite, gold and russet-coloured, and stirred up by the bitter wind – even the hardiest of the beaters succumb to the warmth of the low-beamed, wonky-walled pub for a pint and a pickle, and getting settled in at the bar.

RIEVAULX.10.45AM

An unmistakable sight.
Mid-morning on one of Justin's
organised guest days in September.

GREY-LEGGED, LOCAL SHOT PARTRIDGE WITH BRAISED GREEN

LENTILS, CELERY AND BACON BUNDLES AND FINO SHERRY JUICES

GREY-LEGGED, LOCAL SHOT PARTRIDGE WITH BRAISED GREEN LENTILS, CELERY AND BACON BUNDLES AND FINO SHERRY JUICES

Main course - Serves four
Preparation time: 1 hour
Cooking time: 25 minutes

4 partridges
4 rashers of bacon
4 bay leaves
a little oil, for frying
a sprig of thyme

for the sauce
200ml fino sherry
100ml white wine
1 bay leaf
60g caster sugar
½ litre game stock
seasoning

for the celery bundles
3 sticks of celery, cut into
    1cm x 10cm lengths
2 rashers of bacon
a little rapeseed oil, for frying

for the lentils
400g green lentils [puy]
750ml chicken stock
2 carrots, peeled and
    cut into ½ cm dice
1 stick of celery, finely diced

Preheat the oven to 200°C/ gas mark 6. Soak the green lentils in cold water for one hour, then rinse and place into a pan. Cover with chicken stock and bring to the boil. Simmer for approximately 15 minutes. Add the finely diced celery and carrot just before the end of cooking and cook on for a further 10 minutes.

Take the partridges and place one bay leaf on the crown of each breast, then wrap the remaining rashers of bacon over the top. Place the partridges into a hot frying pan with a little oil and colour all over, then place in the preheated oven for 12 minutes. Remove and allow to rest.

Next prepare the celery bundles. Cut the remaining celery stick into 10cm length batons each 1cm thick. Cut the bacon rashers lengthways and use each strip to wrap approximately 6 batons of celery together. Heat a little oil in a pan and sauté the celery bundles until the celery is lightly coloured. Keep warm.

To make the sauce

Place the sherry, white wine, bay leaf and sugar into a pan and bring to the boil, reducing to a syrupy consistency. Then add the game stock. When the partridge is cooked, deglaze the tray with this sauce, simmering for 3 to 4 minutes, then sieve and check seasoning.

To serve the dish, first drain the lentils and arrange on the plate, remove the legs and breast from the partridge and place onto the lentils with a celery bundle on top of the breast. Place the bacon resting on the legs and pour the sauce liberally around the plate, serving the remaining sauce separately. Garnish with a sprig of thyme.

THE MUCH SOUGHT-AFTER GREY-LEGGED PARTRIDGE EATS REALLY WELL WITH GREEN LENTILS WHICH HAVE BEEN COOKED IN GAME STOCK, ABSORBING ALL THE FLAVOUR. THE FAMOUS PUY LENTILS TAKE ON MOISTURE LIKE LITTLE SPONGES OF GREEN GOODNESS AND ARE DELICIOUS, EVEN EATEN ON THEIR OWN.

RIEVAULX RED-LEGGED PARTRIDGE WITH A 'BEETROOT FONDANT',

CUMBRIAN SPECK, BUTTERED BRUSSELS SPROUTS AND WALNUTS

NIK AND JUSTIN BIRKETT RUN ARGUABLY THE BEST PARTRIDGE SHOOT IN THE AREA, IF NOT THE COUNTRY, AND ARE VERY MUCH PART OF THE SCENERY. THE SOCIAL ASPECT PLAYS A MAJOR ROLE ON EVERY SHOOT, BUT IT WOULD BE HARD NOT TO ENJOY YOURSELVES SPENDING A DAY WITH THEM IN SUCH BEAUTIFUL SURROUNDINGS OVERLOOKING THE ANCIENT RIEVAULX ABBEY.

Main course- Serves four
Preparation time: 10 minutes
Cooking time: 20 minutes

4 partridges
4 bay leaves
100g Cumbrian speck, sliced
a little rapeseed oil, for frying
500ml game stock
1 tbsp redcurrant jelly
12 sage leaves, deep-fried
seasoning

for the beetroot fondant
2 medium beetroots, uncooked
100g butter
400ml game stock

for the sprouts
12 sprouts
16 half walnuts, shelled
seasoning

46_47

RIEVAULX RED-LEGGED PARTRIDGE WITH A 'BEETROOT FONDANT', CUMBRIAN SPECK, BUTTERED BRUSSELS SPROUTS AND WALNUTS

Preheat the oven to 200°C/ gas mark 6. Season the partridges and place a bay leaf onto each breast with a thin slice of Cumbrian speck over the top of it. Seal the partridge in a little oil in a hot pan, then roast in the oven for approximately 12 minutes. When ready, remove from the oven and allow to rest.

To make the beetroot fondant

Peel the raw beetroot and cut into 4cm thick discs. Cover the base of a pan with butter and press the beetroot slices down into it. Cover the slices with hot game stock and place in the oven for 15 to 20 minutes, until tender.

Bring water to the boil in a suitable pan, add a pinch of salt, then blanch the sprouts for 2 to 3 minutes, until tender. Drain and return to the pan, add the walnuts and toss together with a little seasoning.

Take the partridge, removing the speck and place under the grill until crisp. Remove the partridge legs, then the breast from the carcase. Add the game stock and redcurrant jelly to the roasting tray, reduce down to a syrupy consistency. Check seasoning and keep warm.

To serve, first place the beetroot in the centre of the plate, with the partridge legs 'leaning' at the front, and the crown at the back. Alternate 3 sprouts and 4 walnuts at the side of the plate with deep-fried sage leaves on top of the sprouts. Place the crisped speck over the top and pour over the juices. Serve immediately.

RISOTTO OF RIEVAULX RED-LEGGED PARTRIDGE WITH PENNY BUN MUSHROOMS, WILTED 'MATADOR' GARDEN SPINACH AND DODDINGTON'S CHEESE AND THYME WAFER

Main course - Serves two
Preparation time: 10 minutes
Cooking time: 25 minutes

4 breasts of red-legged
 partridge, skin off, 1cm dice
rapeseed oil for frying
1 shallot peeled and
 finely chopped
300g arborio risotto rice
600ml good game stock
a splash of Fino sherry
50g penny bun mushrooms,
 cleaned
100g Doddington's cheese,
 grated
100g matador spinach,
 roughly chopped
50ml whipping cream
50g unsalted butter
seasoning

for the wafers
100g Doddington's cheese,
 grated
a pinch of thyme, chopped

to serve
5ml white truffle oil

In a heavy-bottomed pan,
shallow-fry the diced partridge
in a little oil to lightly colour
for only 2 to 3 minutes, add
the shallot and sweat without
colouring. Add the rice, stir
briefly again, add 500ml game
stock bit by bit, stirring all the
time, so it doesn't stick until
most of the stock has evaporated
and the rice is nearly cooked.

Add a splash of sherry, the
mushrooms, and the cheese.
Check the consistency and
seasoning. The rice should be
'al dente' (firm to the bite), stir in
the spinach, cream and butter.

To make the wafers

Take the cheese and mix with
the chopped thyme. Place four
8cm pastry rings onto a baking
sheet covered with greaseproof
paper. Sprinkle the mix into the
centre of the rings, then bake
in a medium to hot oven for 3 to
4 minutes, or grill until golden
brown. Remove from the heat
and allow to cool and crisp.

To serve, spoon the risotto
into warm bowls, drizzle with
a little white truffle oil and
place a cheese and thyme
wafer on the top.

48_49

THE PARTRIDGE AND PENNY BUN MUSHROOMS ARE A BEAUTIFUL
COMBINATION. THESE FUNGI HAVE A SIMILAR TEXTURE TO
PARTRIDGE AND ARE QUITE 'MEATY'. THE VIBRANT SPINACH
GIVES THE 'POPEYE' FEEL-GOOD FACTOR, AND THE CRISP CHEESE
WAFER IS IDEAL FOR DUNKING INTO THE CREAMY RISOTTO.

SAGE-ROAST RIEVAULX RED-LEGGED PARTRIDGE WITH KILN-SMOKED YOADWATH MILL HAM, CREAMED CELERIAC, SLOE GIN JUICES AND BUTTERED BABY BEETS

Main course - Serves four
Preparation time: 10 minutes
Cooking time: 25 minutes

4 partridges
4 slices Yoadwath Mill
    smoked ham
a little rapeseed oil
1 bunch of sage
125ml sloe gin
16 sloe berries, previously
    soaked in sloe gin
a little butter
250ml game stock
seasoning

for the celeriac
1 large head celeriac
500ml whipping cream
250ml semi-skimmed milk
1 clove garlic, crushed
white pepper and salt -
    avoid black pepper as this
    gives a speckled appearance
    to the celeriac!

for the baby beets
12 baby beetroots
110g butter
a pinch of sugar

Preheat the oven to 200°C/ gas mark 6. Peel the celeriac and cut into small dice. Place in a thick-based pan, pour over the cream and milk and add the garlic. Season generously and bring to the boil, then simmer until tender. Drain off the remaining liquid and retain. Place the drained celeriac into a blender, and gradually add back the liquid, until a smooth, loose consistency is achieved. Season to taste. Keep warm.

Heat the grill and lightly oil a tray. Add the ham to the tray and place under the grill until crisp.

Season the partridges and colour in a hot pan until golden all over. Then place some of the sage leaves into the partridge cavities and place in the oven for approximately 12 minutes, then remove and allow to rest. Take the partridges and remove the legs and the lower carcase to leave the crown. Keep warm and retain the roasting tray juices.

Cut the leaves from the baby beetroots, whilst retaining at least 1/2 cm of the stem on the top. Place the beets into a pan and cover with water, then add 100g butter and a pinch of sugar and cook until tender. Drain and allow to cool before peeling. Place the peeled beets into a pan with a knob of butter and gently warm.

Add the game stock, sloe gin and berries to the roasting tray juices, with a little butter and simmer down until the required consistency is achieved. Check seasoning.

To serve, spoon the celeriac onto the plate, place the partridge onto the plate with the baby beetroot around it and spoon over the sloe gin and roasting juices.

THIS DISH IS A BIT OF A POSH
ONE WITH ITS LOVELY SUAVE
COLOURS AND FLAVOUR
COMBINATIONS. WE USE
THE BOOZY BERRIES, FROM
THE MANUFACTURE OF OUR
HOMEMADE SLOE GIN,
AND SLIVERS OF ANDY
STEWART'S LOCALLY-SMOKED
HAM, A PURÉE OF OUR
NUTTY CELERIAC, AND
GLISTENING PURPLE BABY
BEETS DOTTED AROUND
THE PLATE — THE COLOURS
ARE NEARLY AS DELICIOUS
AS THE DISH ITSELF!

52_53

**SAGE-ROAST RIEVAULX
RED-LEGGED PARTRIDGE WITH
KILN-SMOKED YOADWATH
MILL HAM, CREAMED CELE-
RIAC, SLOE GIN JUICES AND
BUTTERED BABY BEETS**

GREY-LEGGED
PARTRIDGE
AND FOIE GRAS
TERRINE,
CRISP SKIN,
VICTORIA PLUM
JELLY AND
SOURDOUGH
CRISPS

54_55

GREY-LEGGED PARTRIDGE AND FOIE GRAS TERRINE, CRISP SKIN, VICTORIA PLUM JELLY, AND SOURDOUGH CRISPS

Starter/Snack - Serves ten
Preparation/Cooking/
Chilling time: 24 hours

5 partridges
100g duck fat
400g foie gras
6 gelatine leaves
rapeseed oil
seasoning

to garnish
a few herb leaves
    and edible flowers

for the plum jelly
500g plums, halved
    and de-stoned
5g agar agar powder
150g sugar
150g water
150g white wine vinegar

for the sourdough crisps
a small loaf of sourdough bread

Take the breasts and legs off the partridges and roast the carcases in the oven until golden brown. Put the bones in a large pan, cover with water and simmer for 2 hours, then strain the liquid and reduce this down to a quarter of the original quantity. Chill.

Meanwhile, place the partridge legs into a vacuum pack bag with the duck fat and cook for 12 hours at 72°C in a water bath. Place the bag in iced water to chill. Cook the partridge breasts in another vacuum pack bag and cook for 20 minutes at 65°C, then chill the bag in iced water.

Place the plums in a pan with the sugar, water and white wine vinegar and simmer for 1 hour, then strain and chill. Weigh the strained plum juice and add 2% by weight of agar agar powder, then bring the juice to the boil, whisking constantly. Once boiling point has been reached, remove the pan from the heat and skim any froth from the surface. Line a plastic container with cling film and pour in the plum juice to a depth of approximately 1cm. Chill.

Place the foie gras in a vacuum bag and cook in a water bath or bain-marie at 58°C for 40 minutes, chill the bag in iced water, then refrigerate.

To make the terrine

First soak 6 gelatine leaves in cold water, then take 250ml of the partridge stock and bring this to the boil, remove from the heat and whisk in the soaked gelatine leaves. Keep warm. Next strip the meat from the cooked partridge legs and place in a bowl. Pour in half of the partridge stock with the gelatine leaves, and season to taste. Remove any visible large veins from the foie gras and slice into large batons, approximately 1cm square.

Line a standard sized terrine mould with cling film, and add a shallow layer of the leg meat, followed by a layer of whole partridge breasts and foie gras, each time dipping the breasts and foie gras into the remaining partridge stock. Repeat this layering process until all of the partridge and foie gras has been used. Place the whole terrine in a vacuum pack bag, seal and refrigerate.

Freeze a small round sourdough loaf and, without defrosting, slice on a meat slicer on 1.5 or use a very sharp serrated carving knife to cut very thin slices. Place the slices in a large cast iron baking tray, lined with parchment paper, brush with oil and season. Place another sheet of parchment paper over the top, followed by another cast iron baking tray, then bake in the oven at 200°C/gas mark 6, until crisp.

To serve, slice the terrine into 1.5cm slices. Dice the plum jelly into 1cm cubes. Place a slice of terrine in the centre of the plate with the cubes of plum jelly scattered over and around it. Garnish with herb leaves and edible flowers and a few of the sourdough bread crisps.

WARNING: THIS IS QUITE COMPLICATED TO PREPARE.

BORROWED FROM THE KITCHENS OF OUR SISTER HOTEL, THE PHEASANT, JUST 100 METRES FROM US WHERE PETER NEVILLE, MY FORMER HEAD CHEF AT THE STAR, HAS REJOINED US AS A PARTNER IN THE BUSINESS. THIS SILK-TEXTURED TERRINE IS PARTNERED WITH CRISPY DRIED-OUT SKIN AND JELLY, MADE FROM THE VAST QUANTITIES OF PLUMS WE PICK FROM THE ORCHARD IN THE GROUNDS OF THE HOTEL.

Habitual Voyeur

RYEDALE.2.25PM

Originally native to Britain, and dating as far back as 4000 BC according to the archaeological finds that include bones, teeth and antlers. Unfortunately, these beautiful-looking animals were hunted to near-extinction in medieval times, dying out entirely by the turn of the 19th Century. They were reintroduced sometime after the Second World War, at around the same time as the mass replanting of forestry in the UK. They are obviously extremely friendly creatures, as they started breeding prolifically, spreading from Northumberland gradually 'down-country', hence, the vast numbers in our area.

The downside to the increasing number of deer is 'fraying', or constant nibbling of saplings and tree buds, as well as the damage done to tree bark by bucks, the males, rubbing up against trees with their antlers. Does, the females, also manage to create their fair share of mayhem. It might not seem much of a problem, within the thousands of acres of woodland in the UK, but when combined with their insatiable appetite for woodland flowers and other foliage, it all denies food and natural habitats to our native creatures, such as bees, moths, butterflies and birds. As in mainland Europe, where there has previously been a lack of control, the forests and woodlands are now falling ever more silent due to the cull of the deer population.

The 'fairy of the woods', as they are affectionately known, have a canny knack for being there one minute, as the 'keeper takes aim, and then being gone the next, as he is about to pull the trigger, left only with the sound of silence ringing in his ears as another deer dances away into the tree line, disappearing seemingly into thin air...

We get a lot of deer from local estates, where gamekeepers are employed to stalk deer and continuously monitor numbers, in order to stabilise the animals and the countryside as a whole.

Relatively small in weight, at approximately 30-35 pounds (14kg), but big in flavour, deer are easy to handle and quick to prepare, with no trace of fat. All in all they represent some of the finest, moist and flavoursome meat available in autumn and winter months, when this featured 'game' tends to take centre stage.

Roe, Fallow and Red are the most popular, and the most used on our menus. Lovely, delicious and delicate. The Roe is especially abundant around Ryedale, and indeed, Yorkshire.

Park life

Wine Notes - Deer
by Andrew Firth

This is a rich flavour and we need to match up the wine carefully, but, again, personal preference has a big part to play. The flavours you are looking to balance up come from the strong, earthy meat, which is often marinaded. The recipes Andrew has produced all have strong flavours to them. This calls for wines from Piedmont in northern Italy, the home of the Barolo, Barbera and Dolcetto grapes, which match the strength of the flavours of the meat, whilst being quite dry and tannic, so offer a nice contrast. If that's too bold, then, maybe try a Zinfandel from California or a special cuvée from a good producer from the Languedoc, Minervois or Corbières. These have rich, bold flavours, but with a good balance, and, perhaps, best of all would be a Malbec from Mendoza in Argentina.

DEER: THE DARK CRIMSON MEAT IS FULL OF RICH FLAVOUR AND LOW IN FAT. WITH ITS SOFT VELVETY TEXTURE, IT SHOULD BE ENJOYED WITH A DECENT GLASS, OR BOTTLE, OF RED.

DUNCOMBE PARK ROE DEER CARPACCIO WITH YOADWATH MILL SMOKED TROUT, AMPLEFORTH ABBEY 'DISCOVERY' APPLE AND GARDEN FENNEL REMOULADE AND BAKED DILL GRISSINI

Starter - Serves four
Preparation time: 30 minutes
Cooking time: 15 minutes

400g venison loin
5g crushed spices, eg:
    star anise, coriander seeds, etc
a little oil for frying
4 tsp grain mustard
100g mixed herbs, chopped
200g smoked trout, cut
    into 1cm thick slices
a little lemon juice and
    olive oil to finish
seasoning

for the remoulade
2 apples
1 large bulb of fennel
a little lemon juice
50g mayonnaise
seasoning

for the grissini
250g strong flour
5g fresh yeast
$\frac{1}{2}$ tsp salt
$\frac{1}{4}$ tsp sugar
a little olive oil
30ml water
1 bunch of dill, chopped

to garnish
a few fresh herbs

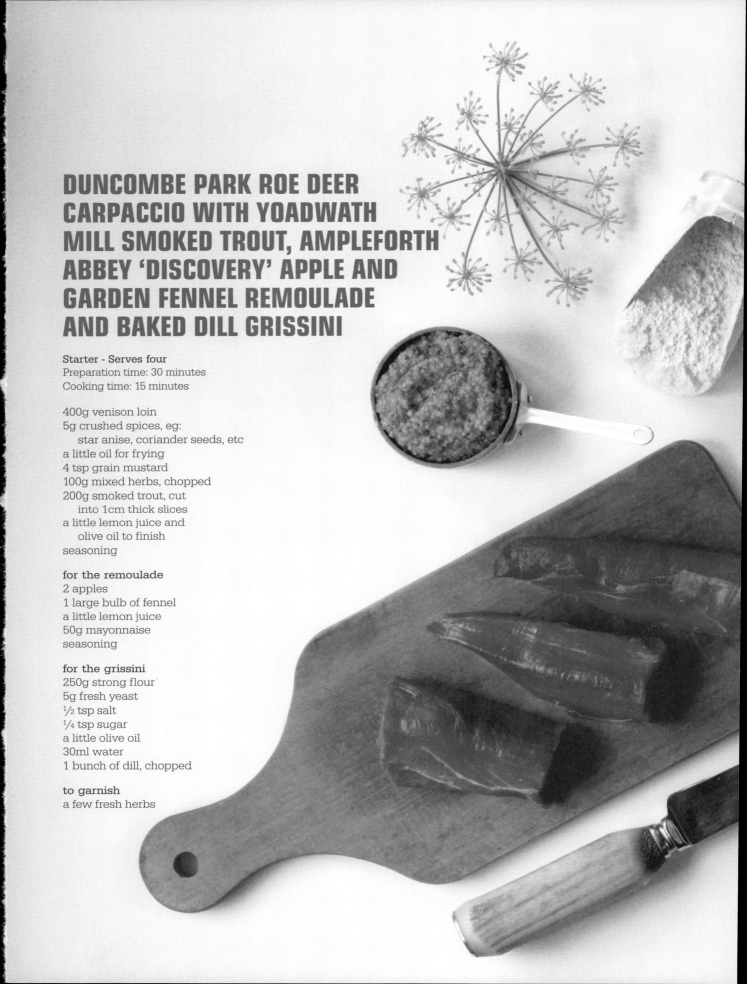

Season the venison loin with salt, pepper and the crushed spices. Heat a large frying pan with a little oil, add the loin and gently brown off for only one minute. Set aside and leave to cool, then coat with the mustard and roll in the herbs. Wrap in cling film to maintain the shape.

To make the remoulade

First peel and grate the apples, then trim and grate the fennel, adding a little lemon juice, to prevent it becoming brown. Season and mix in the mayonnaise to a fine 'coleslaw' consistency. Season to taste.

To make the grissini

Mix together the flour, yeast, salt, sugar and olive oil, then add a little water to mix to a dough. Knead in some chopped dill, cover and leave to prove in a warm place for approximately 20 minutes. Once proved, roll out the dough and cut into thin sticks. Place on an oiled baking tray and cook at 180°C/gas mark 4 for 8 to 10 minutes, or until golden brown.

To plate, cut the venison into very thin slices. Spoon the remoulade into the centre of the plate and then place the smoked trout slices on top followed by the Carpaccio. Then drizzle with a little lemon juice and olive oil, and season. Finish with the grissini and the fresh herbs. Enjoy!

SURF 'N TURF, STAR INN-STYLE! PEPPERED SADDLE OF ROE DEER, THINLY SLICED AND ROLLED OUT, SITS ON TOP OF A TOWER OF AMPLEFORTH ABBEY 'DISCOVERY' APPLES. THE GRATED BLUSHING PINK-HUED FRUIT BRINGS A SHARP TASTE, WHICH IS BLENDED WITH OUR OWN ANISEED-SCENTED BULB FENNEL, WHILST THE DILL GRISSINI GIVES TEXTURE TO THE DISH. LOVELY FLAKES OF SUCCULENT SMOKED RAINBOW TROUT SURROUND THE TOWER, MAKING A VERY SOPHISTICATED SUMMER STARTER OR EVEN A SALAD OR, IN ITS OWN RIGHT, A MAIN COURSE.

DUNCOMBE PARK ROE DEER CARPACCIO WITH YOADWATH MILL SMOKED TROUT, AMPLEFORTH ABBEY 'DISCOVERY' APPLES AND GARDEN FENNEL REMOULADE WITH BAKED DILL GRISSINI

PAN-ROAST HAUNCH OF ROE DEER WITH A LITTLE
VENISON COTTAGE PIE, JUNIPER-CREAMED SAVOY
CABBAGE, YORK HAM LARDONS, HAND-PICKED
YELLOW CHANTERELLES AND GARDEN THYME JUICES

Main course - Serves four
Preparation time: 30 minutes
Cooking time: 15 minutes

for the haunch
4 x 125g venison haunch steaks
a little oil for frying

for the sauce
1 litre game stock
1 tsp redcurrant jelly
250ml red wine, eg: Shiraz
    or Burgundy
2 sprigs of thyme
125g York ham lardons
250g yellow chanterelle
    mushrooms

for the cottage pie
1 medium white onion,
    finely chopped
1 clove garlic, finely grated
a little rapeseed oil
250g minced venison
125ml red wine
4 juniper berries, ground
400ml game stock
2 medium carrots, cut
    into ½ cm dice
a little cornflour
a splash of gravy browning
200g mashed potato with a
    little chopped parsley
    mixed in, warmed
seasoning

for the creamed cabbage
1 medium savoy cabbage,
    thinly sliced
200ml whipping cream
80g Cheddar cheese, grated
6 juniper berries, ground
seasoning

to garnish
4 sprigs of thyme

Preheat the oven to 190°C/ gas mark 5. First prepare the Cottage Pie ingredients, by sweating the onions and garlic in a little oil, without colouring. Add the minced venison to the onions and garlic, and brown, then add the red wine, ground juniper berries and the stock. Season and cook on a medium heat for approximately 20 minutes. Add the diced carrot and cook for a further 10 minutes. Add a splash of gravy browning and thicken with a little cornflour, as required.

Meanwhile place the ingredients for the sauce (game stock, redcurrant jelly, red wine and one sprig of thyme) into a pan and reduce down to ½ litre, to give a dark, syrupy consistency. Pass through a sieve or muslin cloth. Just before serving, gently warm the sieved sauce and add the lardons, chanterelles and a few thyme leaves.

To make the creamed cabbage

First reduce the cream by half, then add the cabbage, cheese, juniper and seasoning to taste, and cook until tender. The mixture should be quite dry so that it doesn't run into the sauce (or serve it separately).

Generously season the venison steaks and fry in a pan with a little oil until a golden colour, then place into the oven for 2 minutes. Remove and allow to rest for 2 minutes.

To serve, place the cooked venison mince into a small ramekin or pan and pipe warm mashed parsley potato over the top. Place under a hot grill to brown. Then take the rested steaks and carve into five or six slices.

Place a bed of the creamed cabbage onto the centre of the plate with the sliced meat on top. Bring the sauce to the boil and spoon around the meat. Finally position the cottage pie by the side of the meat and garnish with herbs or a sprig of deep-fried thyme.

PAN-ROAST HAUNCH OF ROE DEER WITH A LITTLE VENISON COTTAGE PIE, JUNIPER-CREAMED SAVOY CABBAGE, YORK HAM LARDONS, HAND-PICKED YELLOW CHANTERELLES AND GARDEN THYME JUICES

THIS IS ONE OF OUR BEST SELLING WINTER DISHES, POSSIBLY BECAUSE EVERYONE CAN RELATE TO THE 'COTTAGE PIE' ELEMENT. SOMETHING WE HAVE ALWAYS BEEN CAREFUL ABOUT IS MAKING SURE PEOPLE ARE RELAXED AND HAVE A CERTAIN KNOWLEDGE OF AT LEAST SOME PART OF OUR DISHES. THE HAUNCH IS PEPPERED AND PAN-FRIED TO A DEEP, RARE CRIMSON COLOUR, SLICED ONTO THE RICH, CHEESY SAVOY WITH THE LARDONS OF YORK HAM, BASICALLY POSH BACON BITS, AND YELLOW CHANTERELLES, THE 'MUSHROOM OF THE MOMENT' DURING THE AUTUMN AND WINTER MONTHS.

VENISON SAUSAGE 'TOAD IN THE HOLE' WITH PINEAPPLE-BRAISED RED CABBAGE AND PROPER ONION GRAVY

72_73

Main course - Serves four
Preparation time: 40 minutes
Cooking time: 30 minutes

for the Yorkshire Pudding batter
3 eggs
200g plain flour, sieved
200ml milk
pinch of dried herbs
seasoning

for the braised cabbage
1 small pineapple,
    peeled and diced in 1cm cubes
1 large red cabbage,
    finely shredded
100ml white wine vinegar
200g light brown sugar
500ml red wine
2 star anise
1 cinnamon stick
1 tbsp redcurrant jelly

for the Sausages
[or use 500g good quality
butcher-made venison sausages,
if you wish]
25g natural sausage skins,
    soaked in cold water for 4 hours
500g venison, minced
zest of 2 oranges
2 level tbsp mixed spice
1 clove garlic, grated
100g breadcrumbs
1 egg
a little cooking oil

for the Gravy
2 large white onions, sliced
½ litre veal jus

Preheat the oven to 180°C/
gas mark 4.

To make the Yorkshire Pudding batter

First break the eggs into a bowl
and whisk, then add the sieved
flour and the milk, and whisk
again until smooth. Pass through
a sieve to ensure there are no
lumps. Add the dried herbs and
seasoning and leave to 'rest' in
the refrigerator.

To make the braised cabbage

Place all of the ingredients, with
the exception of the pineapple,
into a pan and bring to the boil.
Then, reduce the heat to medium
and cook for a further 20 to
25 minutes, until the cabbage
is tender and the liquid has
reduced to a syrupy consistency.
Remove from the heat, add the
diced pineapple and keep warm.

Next, if making your own
sausages, combine the
ingredients and pipe into sausage
skins. Brown the sausages in
a little oil, in whichever tray or
pan the Toad in the Hole is to be
cooked. Once browned, pour the
Yorkshire Pudding batter over
the hot sausages and place in a
the preheated oven for around
25 minutes, until the Yorkshire
Pudding is crisp and golden
brown, and the sausages are
cooked through.

Meanwhile, sweat off the sliced
onions for the Gravy in a little oil
without colouring, heat the jus
separately and combine shortly
before serving.

Serve the Toad in the Hole with
a good amount of the pickled
red cabbage, and pour over
the gravy immediately before
serving. Add mashed potato,
to the dish, if you wish.

DEREK FOX'S BUTCHERS', LOCATED IN THE PICTURESQUE MARKET PLACE AT MALTON, MAKES
GREAT VENISON SAUSAGES LIKE THE KIND WE USE AT THE PUB. WE MAKE OUR TOAD-IN-THE-HOLE
IN CAST IRON BLINI PANS; A COUPLE OF DECENT, THICK SAUSAGES IN EACH, WITH YORKSHIRE
PUDDING BATTER POURED OVER, COOKED IN A HOT OVEN UNTIL THEY ARE CRISP AND GOLDEN.
THEY ARE THEN SERVED WITH A JUG OF RED WINE-ENHANCED ONION GRAVY AND A DELICIOUS
PILE OF BRAISED RED CABBAGE WITH JEWELS OF GOLDEN PINEAPPLE FOLDED THROUGH IT.
A PERFECT PUB LUNCH ON A WINTER'S DAY!

PAN-ROAST ROE DEER SADDLE
WITH HOMEMADE JUNIPER
SAUSAGE, WENSLEYDALE-CREAMED
CAVOLO NERO, BAKED GREENGAGE
'TATIN' AND STONES GREEN
GINGER WINE JUICES

THE PINK AND DEEP MAROON-COLOURED SLICES OF DEER REST AGAINST THE INKY BLACK BRASSICA OF CAVOLO NERO, WHICH IS FRESHLY PICKED FROM THE KITCHEN GARDEN AND WILTED DOWN. THE WENSLEYDALE BALANCES OUT THE CRISP SWEETNESS OF THE SHORT-SEASON GREENGAGE PLUM 'TARTE' AND THE INDIVIDUAL TASTE OF STONE'S GINGER WINE. IT REMINDS ME OF 'WHISKY MAC' – TIMES GONE BY! ALL IN ALL, A GREAT COUNTER-BALANCE, AND THE SOFTNESS OF THE SAUSAGE, WITH THE HINT OF JUNIPER, MAKES IT A VERY POPULAR AND DELICIOUS DISH.

Main course - Serves four
Preparation time: 50 minutes
Cooking time: 20 minutes

for the sausages
1 chicken breast
2 medium egg whites
4 juniper berries, ground
5g tarragon, chopped
500ml double cream
seasoning [white rather than
    black pepper]

for the saddle
4 x 250g roe deer saddle steaks
a little rapeseed oil for frying

for the greengage tatin
2 greengage plums
200g ready-made puff pastry,
    cut into 6cm discs
1 egg yolk
20g caster sugar

for the cavolo nero
8 cavolo nero leaves,
    roughly chopped
200ml whipping cream
80g Hawes Wensleydale cheese
seasoning

for the Sauce
2g ground ginger
100ml veal jus
25ml Stones Ginger Wine

Preheat the oven to 200°C/ gas mark 6. First prepare the sausages. Roughly chop the chilled chicken breasts into 2cm dice, blend in a food processor until fine, then gradually add the egg whites, bit by bit, then add the juniper and tarragon and finally dribble in the chilled cream as the processor rotates to lighten the mousse. Check the seasoning, then place the mousse into a piping bag. Place a double layer of cling-film onto the table top and pipe a long line of 'sausage', the diameter of a 10 pence piece! Fold over the cling-film and roll tightly. Tie each end and twist into 8cm long sausages (or you poach as one long sausage and cut into lengths later, if you find that easier). Chill the sausages for 30 to 45 minutes, then poach in simmering water for 8 to 10 minutes. Set aside. These will be fried to order or can be used as a separate dish.

Next, egg-wash the puff pastry discs with neat egg yolk, place half a greengage, cut side up on each, sprinkle with sugar, then 'cup' and fold around the plum. Chill for 30 minutes. Then cook for 10 to 12 minutes and keep warm.

Season the saddle steaks and fry off in a little rapeseed oil for 2 to 3 minutes each side, then place in the oven for another 2 minutes. Remove and allow to rest. Keep warm. Add the juniper sausages to the same pan and colour. Remove and keep warm.

Add the sauce ingredients to the same pan, bring to the boil and reduce by one third.

Wilt down the cavolo nero with the cream, cheese and seasoning for 2 to 3 minutes. Finally warm the sauce ingredients together.

To serve, arrange the cavolo nero on the plate, cut the saddles into 5 slices and place on top with the tart and sliced sausage next to it, pour over the sauce and serve immediately.

76_77

PAN-ROAST ROE DEER SADDLE WITH HOMEMADE JUNIPER SAUSAGE, WENSLEYDALE-CREAMED CAVOLO NERO, BAKED GREENGAGE 'TATIN' AND STONES GREEN GINGER WINE JUICES

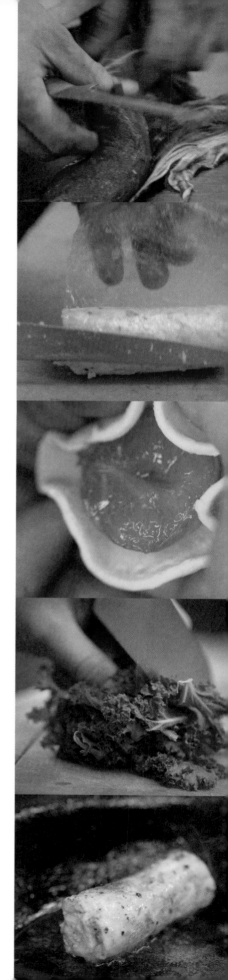

FALLOW DEER PIE WITH LIQUORICE GRAVY, SCOTTISH GIROLLES, RASPBERRY VINEGAR AND CURLY KALE 'COLCANNON'

I WAS AT HOME ONE NIGHT
'IN CHARGE' OF THE KIDS
WHEN THERE WAS A KNOCK
ON THE DOOR. STANDING
THERE WAS STEVE SMITH,
MY HEAD CHEF, AND A PIE!
WE'D BEEN TALKING ABOUT
PUTTING A 'PIE OF THE DAY'
ON THE BLACKBOARD TO KEEP
THE STAR MORE 'PUBBY'
AND STEVE CONJURED UP
THIS CREATION – COMBINING
DEER AND LIQUORICE! IN
YORKSHIRE?! SOMEWHAT
DUBIOUSLY, I TASTED
IT, BREAKING OPEN THE
SHORTCRUST TOPPING TO
THE STEAMING HOT FILLING
INSIDE… AND I MUST SAY IT
IS ONE OF THE NICEST THINGS
I'VE EVER EATEN. I CAN STILL
TASTE IT NOW, A BEAUTIFUL,
DEEP FLAVOUR WITH A SLIGHT
EDGE OF FRUIT COMING
FROM THE VINEGAR, AND
THE VIBRANT MASH TO MOP
UP THOSE LOVELY, LIQUORICE
JUICES. WHO'D HAVE EVER
THOUGHT YOU'D HEAR ME
SAYING THAT? A MUST-TRY-IT!

FALLOW DEER PIE
WITH LIQUORICE GRAVY,
SCOTTISH GIROLLES,
RASPBERRY VINEGAR AND
CURLY KALE 'COLCANNON'

Main course - Serves four
Preparation time: 40 minutes
Cooking time: 2 hours

for the pie
1kg venison, diced
a little oil for frying
16 baby onions
½ bottle of red wine
1 litre game stock
2 cloves garlic, crushed
8 Pontefract cakes
2 tbsp cornflour
1 sprig of tarragon
100g girolle mushrooms
50ml raspberry vinegar
seasoning

for the shortcrust pastry
50g plain flour
30g butter
pinch of salt
cold water

for the colcannon
4 maris piper potatoes,
    peeled and diced
80g butter
20ml whipping cream
80g curly kale
seasoning

Colour off the diced venison meat in a little oil with the baby onions. Fry off until nicely browned, then add the red wine, raspberry vinegar, stock, garlic and Pontefract cakes. Simmer for approximately 1½ hours or until tender. Thicken with cornflour, add mushrooms, tarragon and seasoning, then allow to cool. Place in a suitable pot or pots, and set aside.

To make the pastry

Rub the plain flour and butter together with a pinch of salt, until 'breadcrumb-like', add the water and combine together into a smooth paste. Do NOT over-knead, as it will make the pastry tough. Chill for 30 minutes.

To make the colcannon

First boil the potatoes until soft. Drain through a sieve and mash with a little butter, cream, white pepper and salt. Add the sliced curly kale, which will wilt with the heat of the potatoes and keep warm.

Preheat the oven to 180°C/ gas mark 4. Roll out the pastry with a rolling pin and using a little flour for dusting to a thickness of 3mm. Place over the pots of venison meat mixture and trim so that the rim is covered. 'Crimp' the edges to stick the pastry down and make a little hole in the middle (or use a pot Blackbird!) to let out the steam. Brush the pastry with the remaining egg yolk and bake for approximately 30 minutes until golden brown.

Warm the colcannon and place on the plate with the pie alongside. Eat away to your heart's content!

UCKED

Wood Pigeon is not as sought-after as its largely French-based cousin, the milk-fed squab pigeon, that graces the tables of many a 'Starred' restaurant. These glamorous cousins can usually be found baked in a salt crust, in restaurants such as Raymond Blanc's world-famous Le Manoir aux Quat' Saisons, which is definitely worth a try if you're ever in the area.

FRESHLY PL

Pigeon, wood & squab, are not actually classed as game, falling into the unfortunate category of vermin: pests, that cause massive crop damage in fields of rapeseed and corn in the countryside, and mayhem in inner cities. However, these 'flying rats', as they are affectionately known, actually taste quite fantastic. One bird per person is usually sufficient. The soft, paler flesh is a real delicacy, although, if the 'crop' from their last supper isn't removed from the neck, it causes the flesh to have a bitter taste.

Due to the vast number of birds available on the market, usually, only their breasts are supplied, pre-prepared, to save time plucking. The birds are simply split long-ways, through the breast, and opened up, cutting them from the bone, and then removed from the carcase entirely. As there is virtually no fat, wrapping the breasts in bacon, or crépinette, is always advisable to protect the flesh as it cooks.

PIGEON & SQUAB: PIGEON, AKA 'WOOD PIGEON', IS RED MEAT THAT HAS STRONG, ROBUST FLAVOURS. 'SQUAB PIGEON' IS DELICATE, DELICIOUS MEAT FROM YOUNG DOMESTIC PIGEONS.

Homebirds

88_91

ROAST SQUAB PIGEON, BRAISED BABY GEM LETTUCE, MUSHY PEAS, SMOKED SADDLEBACK BACON AND LEMON THYME JUICES

92_93

PAN-FRIED BREASTS OF LOCAL WOOD PIGEON WITH ELDERBERRY WINE-BRAISED SALSIFY, MEDJOOL DATE PURÉE, BUTTERED REDBOR CURLY KALE AND EARL GREY JUICES

94_97

SALAD OF WOOD PIGEON WITH YORKSHIRE BLUE CHEESE, WARM COBNUT AND RUSSET DRESSING AND GREENGAGE 'SPRITZER'

98_101

WOOD PIGEON, CHESTNUT AND LENTIL BROTH WITH SOURDOUGH BREAD

102_105

PAN-FRIED BREASTS OF LOCAL WOOD PIGEON, CARAMELISED HOME-GROWN FIG TATIN, PRUNE AND BACON ROLLS AND SPICED JUICES

Wine Notes - Pigeon & Squab by Andrew Firth

A bit like partridge, but offering a darker, stronger meat, these will take a Syrah or Shiraz – not a too 'head-banging' Shiraz, but a good, spicy one from Barossa, or even a Chilean Syrah from Apalta. Crozes Hermitage from the Northern Rhone should also do the trick or, maybe, go to South Africa and have Pinotage. The richness of the dishes is balanced in most cases with fruit, so the wine needs good acidity, balanced by lots of fruit. If you didn't want a red wine, then an oaked Chardonnay would hold up or it could be time for one of those special Australian Hunter Valley oaked Semillons, which are delicious.

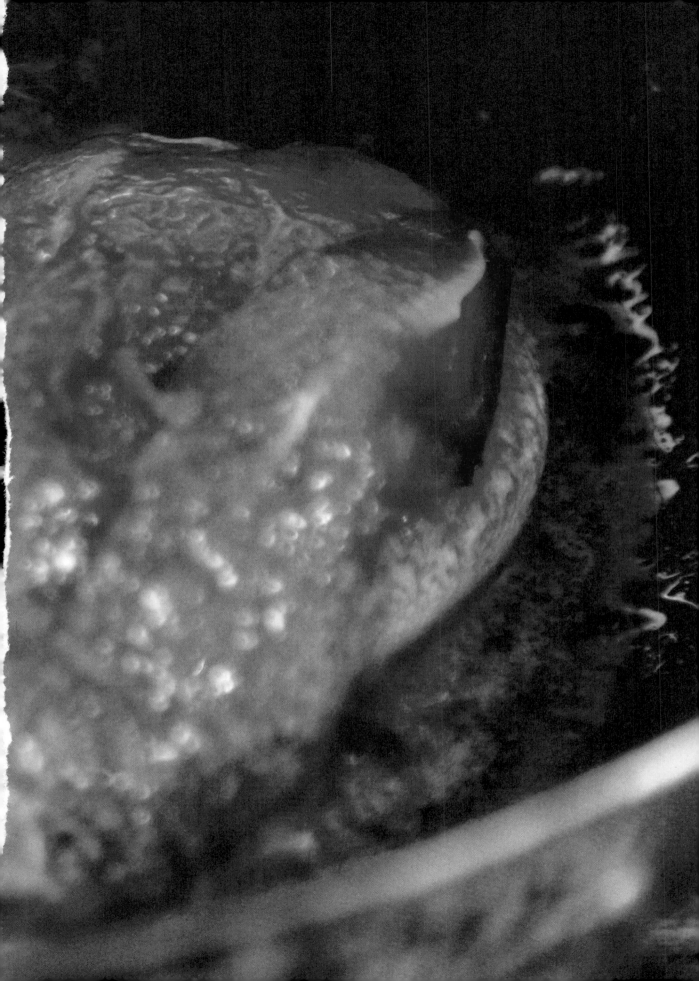

ROAST SQUAB PIGEON, BRAISED BABY GEM LETTUCE, MUSHY PEAS, SMOKED SADDLEBACK BACON AND LEMON THYME JUICES

Main course - Serves two
Preparation time: 30 minutes
Cooking time: 30 minutes

2 whole squab pigeon, dressed
2 rashers of bacon
6 cubes of smoked bacon
50ml Madeira wine
200ml veal stock
20g butter, diced and chilled
2 sprigs of thyme
seasoning

for the braised lettuce
2 baby gem lettuce, cut
    in half longways
a little chicken stock
50g lemon thyme
seasoning

for the mushy peas
200ml chicken stock
200g frozen peas
2 shallots, finely chopped
½ clove garlic, chopped
20m double cream
5g mint, chopped
seasoning

88_89

I LOVE SQUAB PIGEON, AND ESPECIALLY WITH BRAISED LETTUCE AND DEEP, SMOKED SADDLEBACK BACON, WHICH WE LEAVE IN DECENT SIZED PIECES, AND SERVE WITH A PEA PURÉE [OUR VERSION OF MUSHY PEAS] AND A CREAMED, MEATY VELOUTÉ, MADE WITH THE PIGEON CARCASSES AND FINISHED WITH LEMON THYME FROM OUR HERB PATCH. DELICIOUS!

ROAST SQUAB PIGEON, BRAISED BABY GEM LETTUCE, MUSHY PEAS, SMOKED SADDLEBACK BACON AND LEMON THYME JUICES

Preheat the oven to 200°C/gas mark 6. Roast off the dressed pigeons after first covering the breasts with a rasher of bacon. Season and cook for 12 minutes for rare. Whilst these are cooking, gently braise the lettuce halves in a little of the chicken stock and lemon thyme in a shallow tray or pan. Season and cover with foil for approximately 15 minutes.

To make the mushy peas

Bring 200ml chicken stock to the boil, drop in the peas and the finely chopped shallots, ½ clove of garlic. Cook for 4 minutes, then cool slightly and purée in a food processor. Add a drop of double cream and the fresh mint. Check seasoning and keep warm.

Remove the pigeon from the oven, remove from the roasting tray and allow to rest, keeping warm. Drain off the excess fat from the roasting tray, place on the heat and add the bacon cubes, colouring lightly. Add the Madeira and reduce by half, then add the veal stock reducing down by three quarters. Lift out the bacon cubes and pass the sauce through a fine chinois. Return to the heat and bring to the boil. Add a couple of dices of chilled butter and the rest of the thyme leaves. Check seasoning.

To present the dish, carve the breasts and the legs from the birds, spoon some of the 'mushy pea purée' onto the plate, with the warm cubes of bacon and finally the pigeon. Spoon over the sauce, garnish with a sprig of thyme and serve immediately.

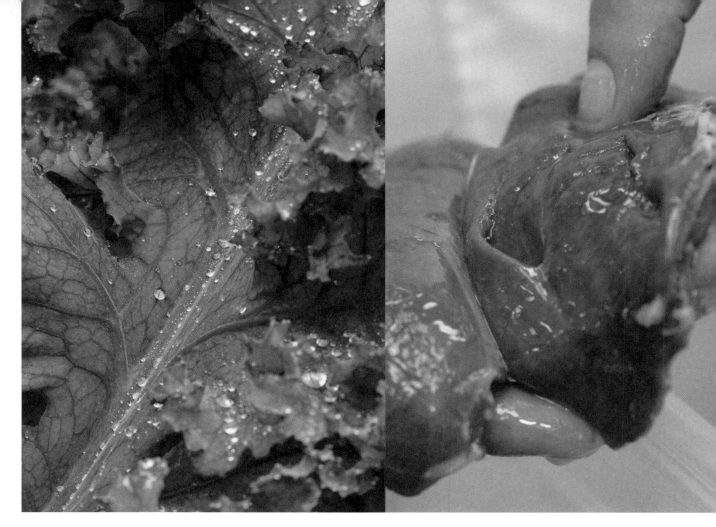

PAN-FRIED BREASTS OF LOCAL WOOD PIGEON WITH ELDERBERRY WINE-BRAISED SALSIFY, MEDJOOL DATE PURÉE, BUTTERED REDBOR CURLY KALE AND EARL GREY JUICES

92_93

THIS IS A LOVELY LOOKING DISH, ALMOST LIKE A PAINTING WITH ALL THE COLOURS TONING IN WITH EACH OTHER: THE RARE PIGEON BREASTS, DEEP PURPLE ELDERBERRY, BRAISED SALSIFY, RED AND GREEN CURLY KALE AND THE DARK, VELVETY TEXTURES OF THE DATE PURÉE.

Starter/Main course - Serves two
Preparation time: 30 minutes
Cooking time: 1 hour

for the pigeon
4 pigeon breasts
8 curly kale leaves
100g butter

for the salsify
2 sticks of salsify
200ml elderberry wine
2 star anise
1 cinnamon stick

for the date purée
500g king medjool dates
10ml Madeira wine
1 tbsp sugar

for the sauce
1 teabag of Earl Grey tea
500ml veal stock
a little chilled butter

for the garnish
shavings from 2 perigord truffles
5ml white truffle oil

Braise the salsify in the elderberry wine with the star anise and cinnamon in a heavy-bottomed pan on a medium heat for approximately 40 minutes.

Cook the dates with the Madeira and a tablespoon of sugar, then blend in a food processor. Pan fry the pigeon breasts in a frying pan for 1 minute each side, then allow to rest.

To make the sauce

First place the teabag into the stock and reduce by three quarters. Add a little chilled butter, check the seasoning and keep warm.

Sauté the kale in butter and place on the plate. Slice the pigeon in half longways and place onto the kale. Add the salsify and shavings of truffle. Remove the teabag from the warm sauce and spoon over. Finish with a little truffle oil and date purée.

SALAD OF WOOD PIGEON WITH YORKSHIRE BLUE CHEESE, WARM COBNUT AND RUSSET DRESSING AND GREENGAGE 'SPRITZER'

Starter - Serves four
Preparation time: 30 minutes
Cooking time: 20 minutes

for the salad
4 wood pigeon breasts
a little oil for frying
150g Yorkshire Blue cheese,
    crumbled
50g cobnuts [or hazelnuts], shelled
100g of mixed leaves and herbs
2 russet apples
50ml olive oil
10ml white wine vinegar
5g grain mustard
5g caster sugar

for the greengage gin
6 greengage plums
25g caster sugar
50ml gin
200ml soda water,
    to make the spritzer

to garnish
a few fresh garden herbs
a couple of extra wedges
    of cheese

94_95

A LIGHT SALAD AS A STARTER OR MAIN COURSE FOR LATE AUGUST/EARLY SEPTEMBER, WITH THE YORKSHIRE BLUE, A SOFT BLUE CHEESE MADE LOCALLY BY JUDY BELL AT NEWSHAM GRANGE, NEAR THIRSK, COMBINED WITH THE SHELL COBNUTS AND NEW SEASON RUSSETS GIVE A 'WALDORFESQUE' FEEL TO THE DISH. AS A LITTLE TIPPLE, WE ADD THE SPRITZER MADE FROM OUR HOMEMADE GREENGAGE GIN AND A LITTLE SPARKLING MINERAL WATER SERVED IN A SHOT GLASS, ON ICE. VERY LIGHT, VERY NICE!

SALAD OF WOOD PIGEON WITH YORKSHIRE BLUE CHEESE, WARM COBNUT AND RUSSET DRESSING AND GREENGAGE 'SPRITZER'

For the greengage spritzer, first poach the plums in 200ml of water and the sugar. Bring to the boil and reduce by half. Leave to cool and infuse, then pass through a strainer. Add the gin, then soda water to the required strength.

To make the dressing

Mix together the sugar and white wine vinegar until the sugar dissolves. Add a little mustard and the olive oil, then whisk to emulsify. Peel and chop the russet apples into small dice and add to the dressing. Heat the cobnuts in the oven at 150°C and keep warm. Just before serving, mix the salad leaves, herbs and Yorkshire Blue cheese in a bowl. Add the cobnuts to the dressing, then add the dressing to the bowl and combine with the leaves and cheese.

Heat a frying pan on a medium heat and add a little oil. Season the pigeon breasts and pan-fry for approximately 1 minute per side, turning as you go to colour on all sides. Once cooked, set aside to rest and keep warm.

To serve, place a handful of the 'salad' into a small serving bowl or onto a small plate. Slice the pigeon breast and arrange on top. Serve with a couple of wedges of cheese and a few herbs. Add the soda water to the greengage gin and serve the spritzer next to the salad.

Note The gin can be done in bulk year upon year, using the same ratios, much the same as you would make sloe gin, depending upon availability and storage space (and gin!!).

WOOD PIGEON, CHESTNUT
AND LENTIL BROTH WITH
SOURDOUGH BREAD

WOOD PIGEON, CHESTNUT AND LENTIL BROTH WITH SOURDOUGH BREAD

Preheat the oven to 200°C/gas mark 6. Roast the pigeon carcases for 10 minutes until golden. Place into a large pan and add the onion, garlic, bay leaves, water and red wine. Bring to the boil, then simmer at the lowest setting for approximately two hours, removing any 'scum' from the surface from time to time. Top up with additional water during this time, if necessary. Once the stock has a strong flavour, remove the bones and pour the stock into another pan, then add the lentils and cook for approximately 30 minutes, until tender. Add the chestnuts and blend in a food processor. Pass through a fine sieve into a clean pan and check seasoning. Keep warm.

Pan-fry the pigeon breasts in a hot pan, until golden all over, then add a knob of butter and cook for 1 to 2 minutes. Remove from the heat and rest for approximately one minute.

Reheat the broth and serve in deep bowls. Slice the breasts and place on top of the broth. Serve with the Sourdough bread. A little pesto or herb oil to garnish would give an extra dimension.

Starter/Snack - Serves four
Preparation time: 2½ hours
Cooking time: 15 minutes

8 wood pigeon carcases
1 white onion, finely diced
2 cloves garlic
2 bay leaves
2 litres water
½ litre red wine
1 kg puy lentils
500g vac-packed chestnuts
4 wood pigeon breasts
a little oil for frying
a knob of butter
1 small loaf of sourdough bread
seasoning

THE SORT OF SOUP YOU CAN STAND A SPOON UP IN, THIS RIB-STICKER IS JUST THE JOB FOR A LUNCHTIME SNACK, AS THE SNOW IS FALLING OUTSIDE. THE CHESTNUTS AND LENTILS, WHEN BLENDED INTO A PURÉE, GIVE A LOVELY SMOOTH TEXTURE AND ARE VERY MOREISH, WHILST THE DICED PIECES OF PIGEON GIVE A DIFFERENT DIMENSION. IT'S REALLY A MEAL IN ITSELF.

**PAN-FRIED BREASTS OF LOCAL
WOOD PIGEON, CARAMELISED
HOME-GROWN FIG TATIN,
PRUNE AND BACON ROLLS
AND SPICED JUICES**

102_103

AFTER THREE YEARS,
OUR FIG TREE HAS NOW
DECIDED TO BEAR FRUIT,
WHICH IS VERY EXCITING
AND, OF COURSE, FREE[!],
SO WE USE THEM TO THEIR
MAXIMUM. THE PAN-FRIED
BREASTS, FIG TART, SWEET
AND CRISPY, AND THE
'DEVIL-ON-HORSEBACK'
COMBINATION OF PRUNES
AND BACON BULKS UP
THE DISH AND GIVES
A FANTASTIC FLAVOUR.

PAN-FRIED BREASTS OF LOCAL WOOD PIGEON, CARAMELISED HOME-GROWN FIG TATIN, PRUNE AND BACON ROLLS AND SPICED JUICES

Main course - Serves four
Preparation time: 45 minutes
Cooking time: 20 minutes

8 wood pigeon breasts
a little oil for frying
20g butter

for the prune and bacon rolls
12 agen prunes, pitted
12 slices pancetta
12 cocktail sticks

for the fig tatin
10ml water
250g sugar
100g butter
4 figs
4 x 8cm discs of puff pastry,
    rolled to ½ cm thick

for the sauce
100g sugar
3 tbsp red wine vinegar
2 tbsp mixed spice
100ml prune juice
250ml game stock
250ml veal jus
seasoning

Preheat the oven to 200°C/ Gas Mark 6.

To make the sauce

Place the sugar, red wine vinegar, mixed spice and prune juice into a pan and reduce to a syrupy consistency. Add the game stock and reduce again to a similar syrupy consistency, then add the veal jus. Keep warm.

To make the prune and bacon rolls

Lay the pancetta slices out flat and place one prune on each slice. Roll up and secure by pushing a cocktail stick through the middle. Grill for 2 to 3 minutes and place in a hot oven for another few minutes to ensure they are cooked. Keep warm.

To make the fig tatin

Place the sugar and 10ml water into four small pans (or one large one to later cut into quarters) and bring to the boil to produce a light, golden brown caramel. Add small nuggets of butter to the caramel and tip into the tray in which the Tatin is to be made. Place the figs evenly over the top of the caramel, with the puff pastry discs over the top. Bake in the oven for approximately 10 minutes.

Take the wood pigeon breasts and pan-fry until brown all over for approximately 1 minute each side. Turn down the heat and add butter to produce a 'foam' and cook the breasts for a further 30 seconds. Remove from the pan and allow to rest for 1 minute.

To serve, remove the tarte from the oven and place in the centre of a warm plate. Slice the pigeon in half longways and arrange 3 of the little 'devils' on each plate. Bring the sauce to the boil and pour over. Serve immediately.

In late winter and early spring, a lot of time and effort is spent burning-off heather on the Moors. Clouds of billowing smoke greet travellers who are heading to the coast over the moorland main roads, towards Sandsend, Whitby and Scarborough. Although it looks slightly out of control, it's an essential part of the game season, and the carefully monitored burning can only be done when the conditions are dry, and the wind is blowing in the right direction. However, Sod's Law normally prevails, and the opposite will happen – wet heather, howling winds, and even wetter heather!!!

Minor things can make or break the start of the shooting season. Vermin, such as foxes and crows, for example, need controlling in early spring to protect the baby chicks whilst the grouse are nesting and rearing their offspring.

The 'Glorious Twelfth' couldn't be more appropriate. The setting of the North Yorkshire moorland, the largest continuous expanse of heather in England, provides many sun-kissed cheeks and pleasantly exhausted souls, after a day in the warmth of the relentless August sun. With the sound of the skylark and golden plovers in the distance, and on the first day of the season, to be in the presence of the coveted noble grouse, you truly feel that you are in God's Own Country.

Driven grouse days see shooting parties hiding away behind heather and peat-clad butts. The semicircular dry stone hideaways, that are scattered across the moors, were built to conceal guns, and act as cover while the flag-waving beaters drive the birds out of the heather. As the grouse are flushed from the hills, they tend to fly twisting and turning, or they catapult themselves from cover hugging the contours of their native moorland. The excitement is enough to raise the blood pressure of even the calmest sportsman.

ri Ous

GROUSE: HEATHER-FED, RUSSET RED, BESPECKLED WITH WHITE. A GREAT-LOOKING BIRD, SOUGHT AFTER AROUND THE WORLD.

Game is a big business around our part of North Yorkshire, where vast moorland stretches over most of the county, offering some of the best grouse shooting in the world.
The one date that sets the country sportsman's pulse racing each year is the twelfth of August, when glorious sunshine over the North Yorkshire Moors marks the culmination of a year's unrelenting work for most gamekeepers. Unfortunately, success in their job is very much out of their hands; the weather plays a major role in Grouse season. If it's cold and wet when chicks are hatching, the young are denied their vital diet of protein-rich insects, which they need to survive during their first four weeks.

HUTTON-LE-HOLE.SUNRISE

GI

Reluctant Celebrity

Wine Notes - Grouse
by Andrew Firth

This is a time for your very best wine. The grouse is the finest of dishes with which to match wine – and one of my absolute favourites! It's really about whether you are Bordeaux or Burgundy. Get the best you can afford and with as much age as possible. If I had to have a preference then it would have to be young grouse with a Pinot Noir/ Burgundy and, as the season goes on, then, maybe, your best bottle of Cabernet/Merlot/Medoc wine from Bordeaux. Other wines from around the world, which would also work, depending on your budget and, I suppose, who's coming to dinner(!), are Chianti Classico, Brunello di Montalcino, both masterpieces from Tuscany, or, for the white wine drinker, perhaps, an Alsace Pinot Blanc or a decent Pinot Gris would work well.

The Star provides the lunches, which are eaten in huts on the Moors, and are usually fairly robust: braised lamb shanks, oxtails, pork chops and the like. We have an eclectic mix of diners and their requirements 'on the moor', from the young guns escaping the city, who tend to be our easiest customers (as their liquid diet from the night before slows things down a bit, and the sustenance required can go either way), to our friends from across 'La Manche', on the 'autre main' who have other ideas.

Their fayre is, of course, gastronomique! They feed on platters of North Sea shellfish, langoustines, oysters, dressed crab and wild, cured Forman's salmon. They have the finest fillet steak from Scotland, for 'steak frites', perhaps with a little touch of Bearnaise, rack of lamb, and of course, the exceptional selection of cheeses from Monsieur Fava, who owns the beautiful Relais and Chateau hotel in Barbizon, located in the Isle-de-France. Each year he comes to the shoot, with the likes of Mr Hermès, Mr Jonan and various Counts and Viscounts from the French aristocracy. They all dine like kings, and that's just for their lunch!!

Truffles, foie gras and lobster are the ingredients of their staple diet when they return from the day's shoot, and, oh yes, a little more 'fromage, peut-être?'

The 'Euroshots' also tend to enjoy the better wine, from the top end of our list, or, slightly annoyingly (as Chef/Proprietor), they invariably bring their own. The French especially make a habit of this, and their élite staff also tend to ensure that each bottle isn't corked and is ready for consumption, if you know what I mean.

They go out shooting in the depths of Farndale, accompanied by the likes of Andy Fawbert, and his 'mutton chops', I'm never entirely sure what the French aristocracy make of him, or his Moors' dialect. Or, vice versa, what the loaders and beaters make of the 'gaily-clad', with the fancy-coloured 'shaving brush' plumage in their hat bands, their matching garters, and the mixed scent of Gauloises aftershave and garlic! There's always a slight breakdown of the language barrier when we're on a shoot, less Franglais, more 'Ay up Marra!' and 'Ça va Monsieur.

'Walking-up' is another form of grouse shooting, where the Guns plod over the Moors, lined up across thick heather, shooting grouse and relying on the skills of their dogs to then find them. The dogs, normally Spaniels or Labradors, pick up the scent 'on point', and then stay motionless until found by the guns or the 'picker-uppers'. Dogs, an integral part of the team who help flush out birds, along with 'flankers' and 'flags', who position themselves either side of the drive to stop the birds escaping, make shooting them slightly easier, if that's possible.

The warm, wild and windswept Wuthering Heights'esque conditions of the honey-scented moors, above Hutton-le-Hole, make the expanse of moorland a breathtaking sight to see. The climate in the height of summer occasionally resembles that of Southern Europe, and the landscape up there is arid and extremely barren, with peat-based tufts of coarse grass everywhere, sitting like hairy 'gonks' dotted amongst flashes of crimson heather. The 'gonks' are a great source of nutrition, and my dad's gundogs love to tear out the grass and chew the roots, getting pleasure and nutrition from the juicy, coarse vegetation.

In the heart of the Moors, you'll come across evidence of the pre-season burning-off period, with sudden patches of crooked, charred black spikes of burnt heather – it looks like some sort of moonscape, with the colour of sky-blue cornflowers pointing to the open skies. This uniquely raw terrain, which the red grouse has made its habitat, is only for the hardiest of souls, and skin, and feathers for that matter!. On our annual pilgrimage, looking over the rolling moors, you can make out the man-made tracks, where 4x4's take a year-round bashing, snaking adder-like, uphill and downdale, through the deep carpet of, now purple, foliage.

NORTH YORKSHIRE MOORS' GROUSE...TRADITIONALLY GARNISHED

I PINCHED THIS DISH FROM MY FIRST BOOK, 'BLACK PUDDING AND FOIE GRAS', AS IT HAD TO BE INCLUDED IN A BOOK WITH THIS TITLE. IT'S A CLASSIC AND THERE'S NO NEED TO MESS AROUND WITH IT. THE RICH SCENT OF THE FIRST-OF-THE-SEASON GROUSE COOKING IN THE OVENS IN THE MIDDLE OF AUGUST, GETS THE ADRENALIN AND JUICES FLOWING. THE AROMA OF ITS HEATHER-FED DIET FILLS THE KITCHEN WITH A DISTINCT SMELL WHICH DEFINITELY MARKS THE BEGINNING OF THE GAME SEASON. THIS DISH RESPECTS THE MAIN INGREDIENT, GROUSE, BEING NATIVE TO THE BRITISH ISLES, AND IT NEEDS NO EMBELLISHING. IT LETS THE NATURAL FLAVOURS COME THROUGH AND IS SIMPLY ROASTED AND GARNISHED TRADITIONALLY. NOTE - PLEASE DO NOT BE PUT OFF BY THE ROBUST SMELL OF THE BIRD, THE ACTUAL MEAT IS NOT AS STRONG AS YOU WOULD THINK. IT IS SO INDIVIDUAL AND TOTALLY DELICIOUS AND, OF COURSE, VERY HEALTHY [APART FROM THE WINES YOU HAVE TO DRINK WITH IT].

NORTH YORKSHIRE MOORS' GROUSE
...TRADITIONALLY GARNISHED

Main course - Serves two
Preparation time: 30 minutes
Cooking time: 20 minutes

2 young grouse
4 slices of streaky bacon
4 sprigs of thyme
4 crushed juniper berries
a little fat for roasting
seasoning

for the game chips
1 maris piper potato, peeled
oil for deep-frying
salt

for the gravy
100ml veal/game stock
a splash of sloe gin
handful of root vegetables
50ml or a small glass of red wine
seasoning

for the bread sauce
2 slices of bread, white
    and crushed
a pinch of mixed ground spice
½ a white onion shredded
    with fresh whole cloves
200ml milk
seasoning

to garnish
local watercress
homemade or good quality
    redcurrant jelly

To make the bread sauce

Place the onion into the milk and bring to boil. Remove from the heat and leave to infuse for approximately 20 minutes, then remove the onion and add the breadcrumbs, spice and seasoning. The sauce needs to be of loose, dropping consistency. Set aside and keep warm.

For the game chips

Take one large frying potato such as maris piper, peel and slice very thinly. Note - This needs to be done before the roasting of the grouse. Take the finely sliced potato and thoroughly rinse in cold water to remove as much starch as possible – this makes the potato crisps crispier! When this has been done 2 or 3 times, pat dry, and deep fry for 2 to 3 minutes, until golden brown. Season with a little table salt and set aside.

To cook the grouse

Preheat the oven to hot! 200°C/gas mark 6. Season inside and out, place a sprig of thyme inside each leg and two rashers of streaky bacon over the breasts of each bird. Colour in a roasting tray with a little clarified butter or duck fat. When sealed on all sides, depending on size, roast for between 16 and 18 minutes. Remove from tray and keep warm. Add the handful of root vegetables into the roasting tray. Scraping any sediment from the tray, tip any juices from the birds into the tray as well as any offal from the bird – this will add to the flavour. Add a splash of sloe gin, the game stock and a glass of light, red wine. Simmer gently for 5 to 6 minutes, pass through a fine sieve into a saucepan, and check seasoning.

Carve the breasts and legs. Arrange the streaky bacon next to the 'bird' on a warm dinner plate. Put a pile of game chips next to the bird with a sprig or two of watercress. Pour any excess juices into the sauce, pour over and serve with warmed bread sauce and a pot of redcurrant jelly. Note - Keep all the carcasses for making a good game stock; you can always stockpile bones in the freezer and make a decent batch when you have a good quantity.

114_115

BRAISED FAGGOTS OF FARNDALE GROUSE WITH A BUBBLE AND SQUEAK RÖSTI AND GARDEN-GROWN REDCURRANT 'GRAVY'

Main course - Serves four
Preparation time: 2 hours
Cooking time: 20 minutes

100g of pig's caul
meat from 2 'old' grouse,
    including offal [liver and heart],
    roughly chopped
2 shallots, peeled and
    finely chopped
1 clove of garlic, finely chopped
5g fresh thyme leaves
a little oil for frying
150g sausagemeat
200ml of game stock
30g fresh redcurrants,
    off the stalks
seasoning

for the bubble and squeak rösti
2 maris piper potatoes
1 carrot
50g bacon bits
50g savoy cabbage
1 shallot, finely sliced
10g butter
seasoning

Take the pig's caul and place in cold water for up to 12 hours. Take roughly chopped grouse meat and offal and blend together in the food processor. Then, fry off the shallot, garlic and thyme in a little oil until soft. Add to the minced grouse and the sausagemeat, and combine together. Season.

Place the mixture into the fridge and allow to set for about 1 hour. Once set, bring the game stock to the boil, roll the meat mixture in to little balls, about the size of golf balls, and wrap these in the pig's caul (you should get three a portion). Once all wrapped, place in the stock and cook for approximately 15 minutes.

To make the rösti

Grate the potatoes and carrot and place in a bowl. Slice the bacon, cabbage and shallot and add to the mix, season with salt and pepper. Then, heat a small frying pan and add the butter, fry the potato mix until golden brown on one side and turn over and cook to the same colour. Once cooked on both sides, drain on kitchen paper.

To serve, place the rösti potato in the centre of a bowl, take three faggots and place on top of the potato. At this time, the stock will have reduced by half, leaving a fine, rich sauce, add the redcurrants to the sauce and spoon over the faggots. Enjoy!

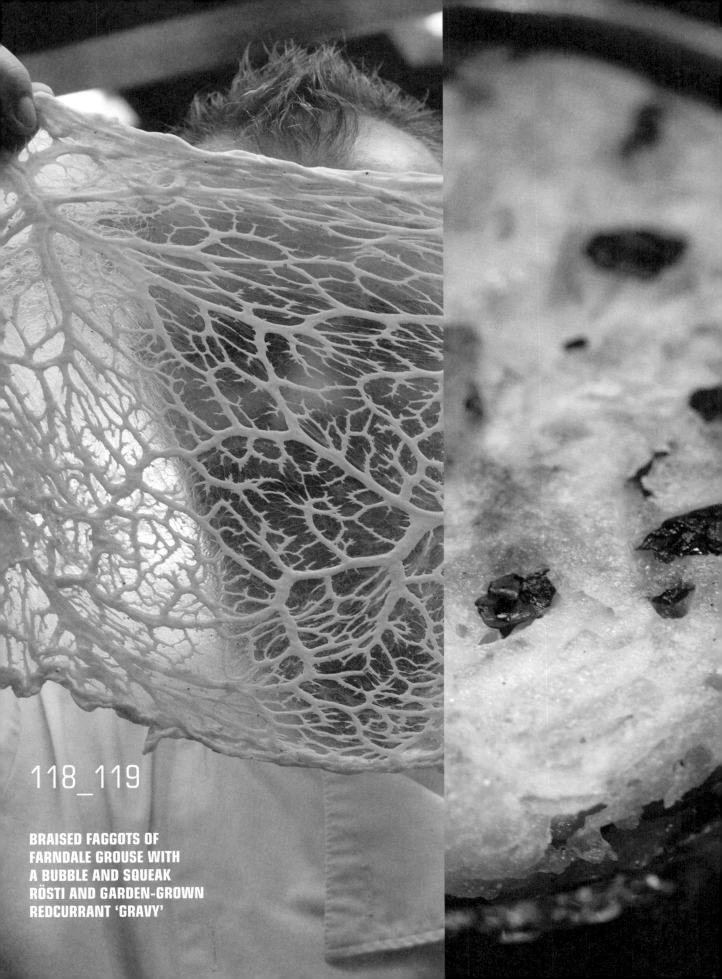

BRAISED FAGGOTS OF
FARNDALE GROUSE WITH
A BUBBLE AND SQUEAK
RÖSTI AND GARDEN-GROWN
REDCURRANT 'GRAVY'

A PERFECT WAY TO USE OLD GROUSE WHICH COULD OTHERWISE HAVE A TENDENCY TO BE A LITTLE TOUGH. WE USE THE LIVERS AND HEART AS WELL AS TO GIVE A GOOD 'OFFALLY' DEPTH. SIT TWO OR THREE FAGGOTS ON A CRISP BUBBLE AND SQUEAK RÖSTI, AND SPOON OVER THE TART REDCURRANT GRAVY – THE REDCURRANTS' ACIDITY HELPS TO 'CUT THROUGH' THE RICHNESS OF THE REST OF THE DISH.

ROAST GROUSE WITH AMPLEFORTH ABBEY APPLE PURÉE, MULLED BRAMBLES AND SLOE GIN JUICES

Preheat the oven to 180°C/ gas mark 4. Place the grouse on an oven tray, season, then take the pancetta and cover over the bird's breasts, to keep them moist, and roast for about 16 to 18 minutes. Then remove from the oven and leave to rest.

To make the apple purée

Main couse - Serves four
Preparation time: 30 minutes
Cooking time: 20 minutes

4 young grouse, oven ready
4 slices of pancetta
3 cooking apples
100g sugar
100ml mulled wine
100g brambles
50ml sloe gin
100ml veal stock
seasoning

First peel and core the apples, then cut each apple into quarters. Place the apples into a small saucepan adding a little water and the sugar, then bring to boil and cook until very soft. Purée in the food processor until smooth.

Bring the mulled wine to the boil, then place the brambles in a small dish and cover with the wine, leaving to cool and take on the flavours of the wine.

To make the sauce

Heat the veal stock and reduce by half. At this point, add the sloe gin, which will add a rich and fruity flavour to the sauce.

To serve, take the breasts and legs off the birds and keep warm, spoon the apple purée on to the plate and place two breasts and legs on each plate, spoon the mulled brambles around the plate and finish with the sloe gin sauce, adding the pancetta to garnish on top.

THIS IS A VERSION INSPIRED BY A LUNCH I ONCE ATE AT LE MANOIR AUX QUAT' SAISONS WITH NIGEL HOWARTH AND A GROUP OF OTHER CHEFS. IT WAS AN EXCEPTIONAL LUNCH, AND WENT ON UNTIL AROUND 8PM [CHEFS WILL BE CHEFS!]. I WAS SITTING BETWEEN TWO LEGENDARY CHEFS, PIERRE KOFFMAN, ON ONE SIDE, AND RAYMOND BLANC ON THE OTHER, AND THE FOOD, THE STORIES AND CAMARADERIE WERE SECOND TO NONE — WHAT A LUNCH!!

BREAST OF GROUSE, BAKED POMMES ANNA, MUSCAT GRAPES AND SWEETCORN VELOUTÉ

BREAST OF GROUSE, BAKED POMMES ANNA, MUSCAT GRAPES AND SWEETCORN VELOUTÉ

Main course - Serves four
Preparation time: 1 hour
Cooking time: 3 hours

4 young grouse
25g butter

for the pommes anna
1kg maris piper potatoes, peeled
250g clarified butter

for the velouté
250g sweetcorn
500ml chicken stock
25g butter

for the sauce
60 Muscat grapes
　　[to make 50ml juice]
50g duck fat
butter
200ml grouse stock
　　[made from grouse bones]
seasoning

to garnish
20 Muscat grapes
watercress tips

Preheat the oven to 175°C/ gas mark 4.

Slice the potatoes on a mandolin to a thickness of 2mm. Place these in a large bowl and pour over the clarified butter. Season to taste. Layer the potatoes in an oven-proof terrine, pressing down each layer firmly, as you go. Once all of the potatoes have been used, cover with parchment paper and bake for 1½ hours. Test the potatoes with a sharp knife at the end of this time to ensure that there is no resistance, then place on a cold tray and use another terrine with weights placed on top, to compact the potato. Refrigerate until completely chilled.

Take the breasts from the grouse and roast the carcases in the oven for approximately 30 minutes, until golden brown. Place the browned carcases in a pan and cover with water. Simmer for 2 hours, strain the stock and reduce to one quarter of the original volume. Put the breasts into vacuum bags, two in each bag, but not touching each other and place on one side.

Place the sweetcorn in a pan with the chicken stock and cook until tender, strain, but keep the liquor. Place the sweetcorn into a liquidizer with 25g butter and blend until smooth, adding the cooking liquor gradually until a soup consistency is achieved. Pass this through a fine sieve, then season to taste.

Halve and de-seed 60 Muscat grapes, retaining 20 for a garnish. Liquidise the remainder and pass through a fine sieve. You will need 50ml of the purée for the grouse sauce.

Place the grouse breasts in the waterbath at 55°C for 12 minutes, then brown in foaming butter in a frying pan and keep warm. To serve the Pommes Anna, cut around the edge of the terrine and warm the bottom until the potato drops out. Slice the potato cake into 1cm thick pieces. Fry the slices of potato terrine in the pan used for the grouse until brown on both sides. Remove the potato and keep warm. Pour 200ml of the grouse stock into the pan with 50ml Muscat grape juice and reduce these to a glazing consistency.

Warm the sweetcorn velouté and pour a pool into the centre of the plate. Place the potato at the top of the plate with the grouse breasts on either side. Place the grape halves over and around and use a little of the grouse stock glaze over the breasts. Finally, garnish with tips of watercress.

WARNING: THIS IS QUITE COMPLICATED!

THIS IS ANOTHER DISH DONATED BY PETER NEVILLE, CHEF AND CO-DIRECTOR OF OUR 'OTHER PLACE', THE PHEASANT, WHO FORMERLY WORKED AT THE TWO MICHELIN-STARRED HIBISCUS WITH CLAUDE BOSI. PETER'S SLANT ON VARIOUS DISHES IS SLIGHTLY DIFFERENT TO OUR OWN MORE CLASSICAL COMBINATIONS, WHICH IS WHAT MAKES HAVING TWO ESTABLISHMENTS GREAT, ESPECIALLY WHEN THEY CAN BE SO DIFFERENT, YET ONLY 100 METRES APART!

'SALMIS' OF GROUSE WITH STUMP

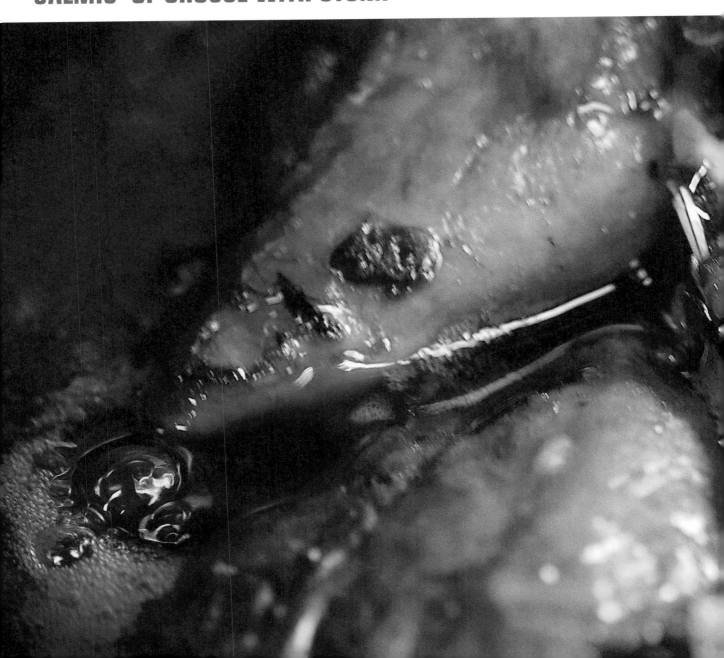

THE SALMIS IS A CLASSIC CASSEROLE DISH, USING OLDER, PERHAPS TOUGHER, BIRDS TO CREATE A WONDERFUL, DEEP, BURGUNDY-RICH STEW. THE STUMP, WITH ITS LESS THAN GLAMOROUS NAME, IS ACTUALLY A YORKSHIRE TERM FOR MASHED CARROT AND SWEDE – JUST ADD A GOOD PINCH OF CRACKED BLACK PEPPER AND YOU ARE AWAY!

'SALMIS' OF GROUSE WITH STUMP

Preheat the oven to 150°C/ gas mark 2. Cut the grouse in half longways, so that you have 4 halves. Heat a little oil in a large saucepan and fry off the breast meat, legs and smoked bacon until browned. Add the diced shallots, celery and carrots, and crushed garlic to the pan, followed by the wine and thyme, salt and pepper, bring to the boil, until reduced by half. Then add the game stock and place into the preheated oven for 2 hours, or until the leg meat is soft and the sauce has thickened slightly (use cornflour, if required).

For the stump

Dice the carrot and swede, and bring to the boil with a little water. Cook until very soft, then drain off the water and mash the carrot and swede, season with cracked black pepper and salt, and add the butter for richness.

To serve, place a leg and some nice chunks of breast in a bowl and cover with the rich red wine sauce and place a good spoonful of the Yorkshire stump next to the casserole.

Main course - Serves four
Preparation time: 30 minutes
Cooking time: 2 hours

2 old grouse (oven ready)
50g smoked bacon cubes
6 shallots, finely diced
2 sticks of celery, washed
　　and diced
2 carrots, finely diced
2 cloves of garlic, crushed
250ml red wine
1 spring of thyme
100ml game stock
5g cornflour, or as required
a little rapeseed oil, for frying
seasoning

for the Stump
6 carrots
1 medium swede
50g butter
seasoning

Because of its reckless behaviour on country lanes, the pheasant has become something of an irritation in parts of the countryside, playing 'chicken' with speeding cars, vans, and even tractors, displaying a worrying devotion to committing suicide or maiming themselves. Headlights, windscreens and wing mirrors are its apparent targeted prey!

'Farmed' pheasant will taste much milder than 'the wild ones' and most other game on the circuit, being similar to farmed chicken in texture.

PHEASANT: BETTER WELL-HUNG, LIKE MOST GAME. COCK OR HEN, A DECENT BIRD WITH ENOUGH FOR TWO.

Walking the Beat

Wine Notes - Pheasant
by Andrew Firth

Pheasant is a bit similar to grouse in terms of wines that work, but, obviously not in flavour. I would not recommend your very best wines and so the new world choices would be a Cabernet Sauvignon from Colchagua in Chile or, perhaps, a Pinot Noir from New Zealand, or a St Emilion or a Rioja – the Rioja goes particularly well with Andrew's smoked pheasant lasagne. And to keep Auntie Lil happy, what about a classical white wine, such as a white Burgundy? To be a bit more radical, a Viognier would go well with the smoked pheasant terrine; it's a slightly richer white to match the richness of the dish.

Service!

It was my grandfather's rifle that (at a far too tender age) I decided to use for a bit of target practice. I placed my old beer cans on the fence, close to Dad's inconveniently parked Triumph 2500 saloon car. I didn't quite have my eye lined up, and started to aim at the McEwan's cans. Yep! you guessed it. The impact of the 'Dum Dum' bullet on the rear wing of the navy blue car wasn't good, as the bullets are designed to explode and spread on impact. Although a huge hole in the bodywork of the car was not ideal, the interior was unfortunately even worse, and, as I recall, so was the exterior of my backside later that day.

I was soon to become a wine consumer (more than a connoisseur!), thanks to my dad's friend, 'Winty'. As he was a 'Wine Rep', he was always chasing new accounts here and there. His company was then a highly reputable wine merchant, covering most, if not all, of Yorkshire. My love of wine was more out of curiosity, and limited to the flavours that suited, or I thought suited, my palate. To this day, I know what I like, and I drink what I want to drink, with whatever food I'm eating. This is not always what I'm supposed to do, apparently. But, anyway, I'll get off my wine-box!

My 'interest' led to Winty setting up my own account, at the age of about fourteen. My dad's name is Alan, so the account was conveniently set up for Mr A Pern. A mixed case of wine appeared once a month. I basically chose the contents because I liked the sound of the names, and the prices!

How was this interest to be funded, you ask? Well, as I mentioned earlier, my mum wasn't able to get about when I was young, so to a certain extent, we fended for ourselves (cooking was never a problem!). Dad in his usual, inimitable way, decided to let us keep our own 'Family Allowance', to buy bits and bobs, clothing etc. I was forever being dispatched to Whitby to buy new school trousers, but I could never find any that fitted, or that I liked (I never was very fashion-conscious). I cleverly decided to re-invest this money elsewhere, thus securing funding for my wine account. So, it was the Government who were actually paying for my box of booze every month, even though I was just fourteen. My school trousers were left with the knees hanging out, and were constantly at half mast, term after term, year after year.

The perfect glass of gently-warmed red wine is a lovely accompaniment to the old roast 'Fez'. The smell of smoked bacon, draped over the breasts of the bird, being slowly cooked and crisping gently, basting the gamey meat as it roasts, is an almost steely erotic smell. These aged birds deserve a glass or two for consumption.

I think I was about 13 or 14 years old when my knowledge, or curiosity, of wine was aroused by David Winterschladen, a lifelong friend of my dad (and me), who has now unfortunately gone to the great wine cellar in the sky. 'Winty', in those days worked for a local wine merchants, 'Yorkshire Fine Wines'. He always had a story to tell, a joke, or gossip on what's happening in 'the trade'. When I was young, he used to call me 'Bocuse', after the world-famous three Star chef Bocuse, or 'Chef of the Century', as he was also known – no pressure then...!

My mother has had MS for a long time, so when I was a child she was largely housebound. Dad, on the other hand, was always out with his rough shoot on the farm. This was a big hit with the local professions (butchers, fishmongers and the like) who all swapped their fine produce for a few days' shooting in the Esk Valley. I was the younger brother, so, by default, I ended up staying in the warmth of the kitchen with my mum at Bank House Farm, on the Aislaby side of Whitby. The aroma of roasts from the oven, or simmering casseroles on the stove, and a good selection of cheese on the sideboard were much more appealing than the harsh outdoors of the farm. Being out in the pouring rain with my hand stuck up a sheep's a*se, or being in the warmth of the kitchen was a no-brainer - and funnily enough, it still is now!!

Although, as a ten year old, the shooting also seemed very exciting. The banter of the characters involved, all the necessary preparations, making sure Dad had enough cartridges to last the day, the sleek barrels of the guns, the sweet, almost addictive smell of the 3-in-1 oil, and the blue-ish tinge of the cleaned and polished side-by-sides all contributed to its appeal. It was always a mystery to us as to where Dad kept the key to the old gun cabinet. I remember, the guns were hanging in the corner of our dining room. I think there were two 12 bores, an air rifle, which my brother and I used, and an old .22 rifle, which my grandfather apparently brought from Belgium during the Second World War – ask no questions!

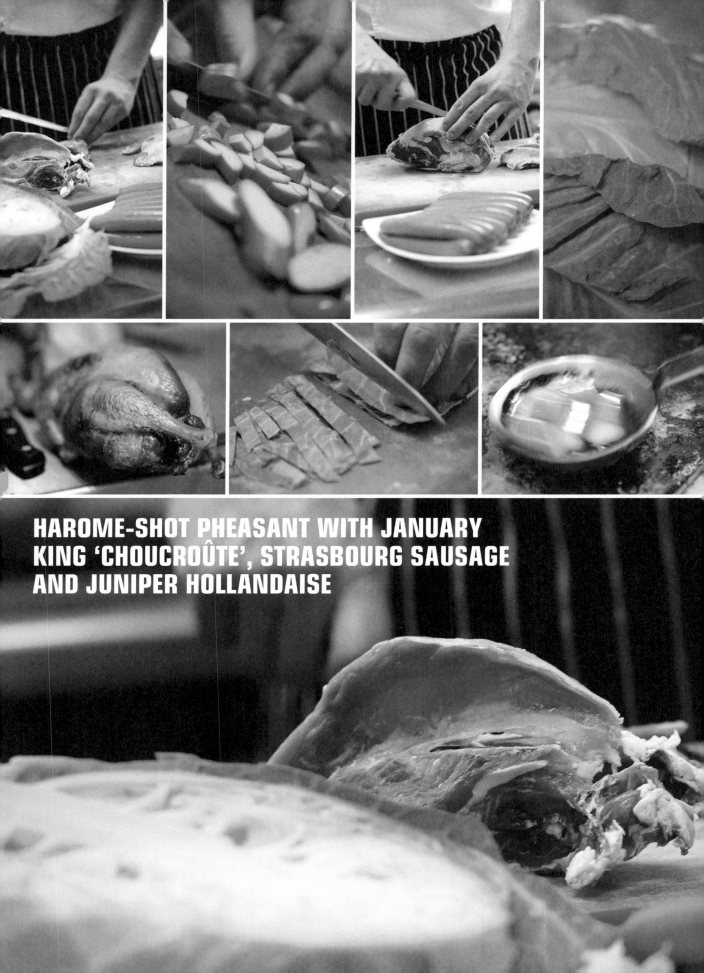

HAROME-SHOT PHEASANT WITH JANUARY KING 'CHOUCROÛTE', STRASBOURG SAUSAGE AND JUNIPER HOLLANDAISE

ROAST PHEASANT WAS ONE OF THE FIRST DISHES I REALLY REMEMBER FROM CHILDHOOD. IT WAS A PROPER MEAL, SOMETHING DIFFERENT FROM THE NORM, ALTHOUGH IT WAS LATER TO BECOME THE NORM! MY DAD HAD A ROUGH SHOOT ON THE FARM, THUS WE HAD A GARAGE AND FREEZER FULL OF PHEASANTS! THE JANUARY KING CABBAGE IS COOKED BASICALLY IN A VINEGAR CONCOCTION, WHICH BLENDS WITH THE BRIGHT RED CONTINENTAL-STYLE 'HOT DOG' SAUSAGE AND IS FINISHED WITH THE JUNIPER HOLLANDAISE. IT'S A HEAVENLY COMBINATION!

HAROME-SHOT PHEASANT WITH JANUARY KING 'CHOUCROÛTE', STRASBOURG SAUSAGE AND JUNIPER HOLLANDAISE

Main course - Serves four
Preparation time: 30 minutes
Cooking time: 30 minutes

2 oven-ready pheasants,
    each covered with a
    rasher of bacon
2 Strasbourg sausages,
    cut in half longways
a glass of red wine

for the hollandaise
200g butter
3 egg yolks
100ml white wine vinegar
5 black peppercorns
1 bay leaf
1 shallot, chopped
4 juniper berries, crushed

for the choucroute
1 january king cabbage
2 juniper berries, crushed
200ml white wine vinegar,
    reduced by 1/3
25g sugar
1 shallot, sliced
seasoning

to garnish
16 sage leaves, deep-fried

Preheat the oven to 180°C/ gas mark 4. Roast the pheasants for about 25min, then leave to rest.

To make the hollandaise

Take the egg yolks and place in a glass bowl. Bring 50ml of the white wine vinegar to the boil with the bay leaf, black peppercorns and 1 chopped shallot added, and reduce by half. Melt the butter in a pan to clarify. Place the glass bowl with the egg yolks over a pan of boiling water and whisk. Add the vinegar reduction and some of the crushed juniper berries, then slowly add the butter whisking until the sauce thickens.

Slice the cabbage and blanch in boiling water for 1 min. Refresh in ice-cooled water to retain to colour. Make a second vinegar reduction adding a little sugar to take the sharpness away. Place the cabbage in a bowl with a little sliced shallot. Season, then pour the hot vinegar over the cabbage with the rest of the juniper. Keep warm.

Portion the pheasant with a little breast and thigh per person. Fry the halves of sausage in the tray used for roasting the pheasants and keep warm. Add a glass of red wine to deglaze the tray and make a 'gravy'. Place the cabbage onto a warm plate with the pheasant, then the sausage on top. Pour over a little of the roasting juices and wine. The hollandaise can be used to finish or can be served separately. Garnish with the sage leaves.

SMOKED PHEASANT, SAVOY CABBAGE AND BEETROOT TERRINE WITH WALNUT AND QUINCE DRESSING

First, line a standard sized buttered terrine mould with clingfilm. Heat the duck fat in a heavy-bottomed pan, keeping at a temperature of 100-130°C. Place the pheasant breast into the fat and cook for 1 hour. Slice each breast into 3 and keep warm.

Soak the leaf gelatine in cold water. Heat the butter and add the soaked gelatine, whisking until the mixture emulsifies. Dip the pheasant breast pieces into the butter/gelatine mixture and place a layer into the terrine. Repeat the process with the savoy cabbage, beetroot, then with the pheasant breast, cabbage and beetroot again, and so on. Place another layer of clingfilm over the terrine and press overnight.

To make the dressing

Mix the white wine vinegar with the sugar, until the sugar dissolves, add the mustard and whisk in the oil. Add the walnuts and chopped quince.

When ready to serve, slice the terrine and place a slice in the centre of the plate, drizzle the dressing around and garnish with fresh garden herbs.

Starter - Serves four
Preparation time: 1 hour
[pressed overnight]
Cooking time: 10 minutes

for the terrine
6 cold-smoked pheasant breasts
4 large savoy cabbage
    leaves, blanched
2 large beetroot, cooked
    and peeled and cut
    into 1cm discs
2 gelatine leaves
200ml duck fat
250g butter

for the dressing
75g walnuts, chopped
1 quince, diced into
    small pieces
2 tsp grain mustard
50ml walnut oil
10g caster sugar
15ml white wine vinegar
seasoning

to garnish
fresh garden herbs

140_141

FOR ME, THE RICH COLOURS AND TEXTURES OF THIS TERRINE ARE 'AUTUMN ON A PLATE'. THE TERRINE INGREDIENTS ARE FIRST COOKED TO PERFECTION, THEN IT IS SET AND PRESSED. IT HAS GAINED RAVE REVIEWS FROM ONE OF OUR MAJOR NATIONAL NEWSPAPERS. IT'S A COMPLEX RECIPE, BUT WELL WORTH ALL THE HASSLE.

PAN-FRIED BREAST OF PHEASANT WRAPPED IN SMOKED SADDLEBACK BACON WITH CHESTNUT MASH, BLACK TRUMPET MUSHROOMS AND PERIGEAUX TRUFFLE

PAN-FRIED BREAST OF PHEASANT WRAPPED IN SMOKED SADDLEBACK BACON WITH CHESTNUT MASH, BLACK TRUMPET MUSHROOMS AND PERIGEAUX TRUFFLE

Main course - Serves four
Preparation time: 30 minutes
Cooking time: 30 minutes

4 pheasant breasts,
    skin removed
4 rashers of smoked
    saddleback bacon
60ml red wine
120ml game stock
1 tsp redcurrant jelly
75g black trumpet mushrooms
20g butter, plus a little
    for the sauce
1 small Perigeaux truffle,
    thinly sliced
a little oil for frying
seasoning

for the mash
200g mashed potato
150g chestnuts
5g chopped tarragon

to serve
wilted winter greens

Wrap the pheasant breasts in the smoked bacon and season. Pan-fry the breasts in a little oil for approximately 8 minutes, then allow to rest. Return the pan to the heat and deglaze with the red wine, then add the stock and redcurrant jelly and reduce. Add a knob of butter to thicken and keep warm.

Fry the mushrooms in a little butter, until soft, and reheat the mashed potato in a small saucepan. Crush the chestnuts and add to the potato, and mix together. Add the tarragon. Pipe some of the mixture onto the plate and arrange cooked pheasant breast onto it. Drizzle a little sauce around the plate and finish with the mushrooms, thin slices of the black truffle and a few wilted winter greens.

THIS DISH WAS ON ONE OF OUR VERY FIRST WINTER MENUS, ALTHOUGH MAYBE NOT WITH THE TRUFFLE IN IT. IN OUR EARLY DAYS! THE CHEAPNESS OF THE PHEASANT DOES ALLOW MORE GENEROUS EXPENDITURE ON OTHER GLAMOROUS INGREDIENTS. USE VAC-PAC CHESTNUTS FOR EASE, OR PARIS BROWN MUSHROOMS AS A GOOD ALTERNATIVE.

SMOKED PHEASANT LASAGNE WITH ROAST HAZELNUTS, CAVOLO NERO, HEDGEHOG MUSHROOMS AND A SALAD OF SWALEDALE BLUE AND PICKERING WATERCRESS

146_147

ANDY STEWART FROM YOADWATH MILL, NEAR KIRKBYMOORSIDE, COLD-SMOKES OUR PHEASANTS SO THAT THEY REMAIN JUICY WHEN COOKED. WE TEND TO DO INDIVIDUAL LASAGNE PORTIONS, ALTHOUGH ONE LARGE ONE FOR THE WHOLE TABLE CAN BE EQUALLY SUCCESSFUL. SERVE THE SALAD SEPARATELY, ON THE SIDE.

SMOKED PHEASANT LASAGNE WITH ROAST HAZELNUTS, CAVOLO NERO, HEDGEHOG MUSHROOMS AND A SALAD OF SWALEDALE BLUE AND PICKERING WATERCRESS

Starter - Serves four
Preparation time: 20 minutes
Cooking time: 10 minutes

4 shallots, finely chopped
1 clove of garlic, crushed
4 cold-smoked pheasant
    breasts, thinly sliced
100g hedgehog mushrooms,
    sliced
200ml cream
40g hazelnuts
4 cavolo nero leaves, sliced
10 sheets of fresh lasagne,
    cooked and kept warm
50g Swaledale Blue cheese,
    grated
a little oil for frying
seasoning

for the Salad
100g Swaledale Blue cheese,
    crumbled
1 bunch of watercress
20ml house vinaigrette
a few croutons and garden herbs

to garnish
a few whole hedgehog
    mushrooms cooked in a little oil

Preheat the oven to 160°C/ gas mark 3. In a large saucepan, fry off the shallots and garlic in a little oil until soft, then add the pheasant and the mushrooms, cook for 4 minutes, then add the cream. Reduce by a half, then mix in the hazelnuts and the cavolo nero leaves. Check seasoning.

Spoon one third of the mixture into an ovenproof dish, then add a layer of lasagne, repeat to fill the dish, ending with a layer of lasagne. Sprinkle cheese over the top and place under a grill for 4 to 5 minutes.

To make the salad

Dress the watercress in a little house vinaigrette, the crumbled cheese and a few croutons

Place the lasagne on the plate and add the salad alongside, along with a few whole hedgehog mushrooms.

148_149

POTTED HAROME-SHOT PHEASANT WITH PISTACHIO NUTS, CORNICHONS AND RUSTIC BREAD TOASTS

Starter/Snack - Serves four
Preparation time: 1 hour
Cooking time: 3 hours,
plus chilling time

1 whole, oven-ready pheasant
   with offal
400ml game stock
200g softened butter
120g clarified butter
75g peeled pistachio nuts
1 pinch nutmeg
200g mirepoix of root vegetables
   [carrot, celery and onion,
   all roughly chopped]
a splash of brandy
50g cornichons, chopped
   very finely
seasoning

for the rustic bread toasts
2 rashers smoked bacon,
   cooked and finely chopped
125g plain flour
40g unsalted butter
4g salt
2.5g sugar
40ml milk
1 small whole egg and 1 yolk
7.5g yeast
10g sage, chopped
1 egg mixed with a splash
   of milk for the eggwash

to serve
50g cornichons

Preheat the oven to 180°C/
gas mark 4. Season the bird.
Add a knob of the softened butter
to a heavy casserole dish, add
the mirepoix of vegetables and
lay the birds on top. Cover with
the stock and cook for about 2½
hours until the flesh is starting to
come away from the bone.

Remove the birds from the dish
retaining the cooking liquor,
allow to cool a little, then strip
the meat from the bone, shredding
into small pieces. Alternatively,
use a food processor on 'pulse'
to achieve the same effect.
Mix the remaining softened
butter, chopped cornichons,
nuts, nutmeg and brandy along
with a little of the cooking liquor,
check the seasoning and adjust,
as necessary. Spoon the mixture
into small kilner jars, ramekins or
glasses, then refrigerate. After a
little time in the fridge, pour over
the clarified butter and leave to set.

**To make the rustic
bread toasts**

A smoked bacon brioche or
rye bread goes well with this
potted pheasant.

Preheat the oven to 180°C/
gas mark 4. Place all ingredients
in a large mixing bowl and
combine together, stirring for
around 10 minutes. Cover the
bowl with clingfilm and leave
to prove for approximately 20
minutes. Roll and place into a
greased 25cm loaf tin, and brush
the top with the eggwash.
Allow to prove again in a warm
place, covered with clingfilm,
then place into the preheated
oven and cook for approximately
45 minutes. To check that the
brioche is cooked, tap on the
bottom of the tin and the sound
should be 'hollow'. Turn out
onto a rack and allow to cool.

Serve with warm toasts and a
little pile of cornichons.

152_153

**POTTED HAROME-SHOT
PHEASANT WITH PISTACHIO
NUTS, CORNICHONS AND
RUSTIC BREAD TOASTS**

A PERFECT SNACK OR STARTER ON A COLD WINTER'S
DAY, THIS HAS THE STYLE OF A FRENCH 'RILLETTE' WITH
SHREDDED-DOWN MEAT SET IN DUCK FAT, SEMI-CRUSHED
PISTACHIO NUTS AND VINEGARY CORNICHONS TO CUT
THROUGH THE FATTINESS, WHICH ALL GOES WELL WITH
THE WARM RUSTIC TOASTS. IT CAN BE USED WITH VARIOUS
GAME, PARTRIDGE, GROUSE AND VENISON BY TWEAKING
THE RECIPE AND USING A LITTLE IMAGINATION.

E HEAT°

CHEF'S TABLE.6.45PM

Located to one side of our main
kitchen in a panelled dining room,
the Chef's Table seats up to eight
guests and combines 'behind the
scenes' views with the opportunity
of seeing dishes being prepared for
your own party and actually getting
involved, if you wish.

CHICKEN: SHE'S A BIRD WITH WIDE APPEAL, VERY VERSATILE,
AND VERY MUCH LOVED FOR HER SUCCULENT SKIN, AMPLE
BREASTS, TENDER THIGHS AND DELICIOUS DRUMSTICKS.
A GREAT ALL-ROUNDER FOR ANY OCCASION.

TURN UP TH

Pecking Order

160_163

**POTTED 'LOOSE BIRDS'
CHICKEN LIVER AND FOIE
GRAS PARFAIT, SALAD
OF SPICED LIVERS AND
'GOOSEGOG' RELISH**

164_167

**HAY-BAKED 'LOOSE BIRDS'
CHICKEN WITH SWALEDALE-
BAKED DAUPHINOISE,
SMOKED SADDLEBACK
BACON ROLLS AND
BUTTERED SPINACH**

168_171

**CHICKEN 'HOTCH POTCH'
WITH STAR INN KITCHEN
GARDEN VEGETABLES**

172_175

**'LOOSE BIRDS' CHICKEN,
HAWES WENSLEYDALE AND
HAMBLETON ALE PIE**

176_177

**BALLOTINE OF CORN-FED
CHICKEN, YORK HAM AND
FOIE GRAS, PICKLED BLACK
TRUMPET MUSHROOMS,
SAGE AND SHALLOT BRIOCHE
AND YORKSHIRE RELISH**

**Wine Notes - Chicken
by Andrew Firth**

The choice here would be totally
down to the dish and type of
chicken, with more expensive
dishes deserving a corresponding
wine. Obviously, chicken is a fairly
light meat so the wines should be
lighter, and a bit different. A red
Sancerre (Pinot Noir) or Chinon
(Cabernet Franc) from the Loire
valley are both good, but may be
a little expensive, so for everyday
consumption, choose a Beaujolais
Villages (Gamay) or a Merlot from
Chile or France, or a red Bordeaux
for that matter, from a lighter, 'less
good' vintage, which will therefore
be cheaper! White wine choices
would include Chenin Blanc from
South Africa, a grapey medium-
weight wine with good fruit, or a
'blast from the past', Entre-deux-
Mers, a white Bordeaux.

If you compare the 'VIP' to the outdoor-reared variety, such as our very own 'Loose Birds', supplied from the outskirts of our village, they're not a million miles away. Our 'Loose Birds' have a similar tight texture, but with a deeper colour, due to the corn, and have larger breasts, tailored to the English market. They're free to roam the countryside, and reared in sawdust-laden, warmed pens (resembling shanty towns), that are made up from a mix 'n' match of sheds and old articulated wagon trailers, surrounded by a lot of mud, with an abundance of clean Yorkshire air. As birds grow, they move along the line of ramshackle sheds, like a type of poultry death row, facing a certain inevitability as they reach the last one.

This process is, unfortunately, limited to the minority of poultry farmers, the others using battery processing techniques, producing 'plastic' chickens and ancillary products that fill most supermarket shelves. In a lot of cases, chickens are poorly reared, pumped full of water, and frozen down to weigh more. The result of their poor diet produces a poor product, and a poor meal. So, how lucky are we, that we don't all have to use that kind of rubbish?

Paul Talling is, as we call him, 'the chicken man', who owns the poultry and game company in our village, that supplies us with 'Loose Birds'. He set up the company over a decade ago, to utilise game from local shoots and estates of the North Yorkshire Moors and surrounding farmlands, providing the 'crème de la crème' of 'Loose Birds and Game', prepared to an impeccable standard. He also supplies outdoor-reared 'Poulet Anglais' chickens, and a cross of Pekin and Aylesbury duck, which have been much sought after by Michelin-Starred chefs from around the country. Paul is one of our 'Star' suppliers, with whom I have always enjoyed a great working relationship. On many occasions, we've put together an order over a pint or two, and the next morning I've wondered where the hell all those ducks and chickens have come from...

Everyone's favourite, the good old chuck! Like most things in life, you have 'the good', 'the bad', and, even 'the ugly'!

The good, of course, is the best, or the 'VIP', the Very Important Poulet, as Simon Hopkinson describes it in his exceptional piece of literature 'Roast Chicken and Other Stories', referring to the French variety from Bresse, said to be the finest chicken in the world. It has a beautiful depth of flavour and is firm-fleshed, with a shape resembling a game bird, and it has longer legs, and slimmer breasts than a 'normal' chicken. It's also hung to develop the flavour.

POTTED 'LOOSE BIRDS' CHICKEN LIVER AND FOIE GRAS PARFAIT, SALAD OF SPICED LIVERS AND 'GOOSEGOG' RELISH

POTTED 'LOOSE BIRDS' CHICKEN LIVER AND FOIE GRAS PARFAIT, SALAD OF SPICED LIVERS AND 'GOOSEGOG' RELISH

Starter/Snack - Serves ten
Preparation time: 1 hour
Cooking time: 1½ hours plus
chilling time

for the parfait
100ml port
100ml brandy
150g shallots, sliced
3 cloves of garlic, crushed
1 sprig of thyme
200g foie gras
200g chicken livers
4 eggs
400g butter, melted

for the salad
100g chicken livers
20g plain flour
10g chilli powder
10g mixed spice
seasoning

for the relish
1kg gooseberries
1 onion, finely chopped
50g caster sugar
5tsp white wine vinegar
10g green peppercorns

to serve
a few garden herb flowers
dressed salad leaves
Poîlane rye bread toasts

162_163

WE CHEAT SLIGHTLY ON THIS DISH BY MAKING THE PARFAIT IN TERRINE MOULDS, THEN PIPING IT INTO SOME NIFTY LITTLE JARS, ESSENTIALLY FOR PRESENTATION, BUT IT WOULD BE FINE TO LEAVE IT IN THE MOULD FOR THE TABLE. 'GOOSEGOG' IS JUST ANOTHER COUNTRY TERM FOR GOOSEBERRIES AND POILÂNE IS JUST THE BEST RYE BREAD IN THE WORLD!

Preheat the oven to 160°C/ gas mark 3 and have a terrine or pâté mould ready.

Place the port and brandy into a pan with the shallots, garlic and thyme and bring to the boil. Reduce down considerably to a glazing consistency and remove the thyme. Slice the foie gras and chop the livers. Place these into a warm pan and heat to a temperature of approximately 40°C. Place the livers, foie gras and shallot mixture into a liquidizer and blend until smooth. Add the eggs and mix well, then add the warmed butter to the mixture and pass the whole lot through a fine sieve. Transfer to a standard sized terrine mould and cover with foil. Place the terrine in a bain-marie and cook for 45 minutes to 1 hour at a temperature of 110°C. Once cooked, remove from the bain-marie, allow to cool, then refrigerate for 12 hours.

Remove the parfait from the mould and spoon into a piping bag. Pipe the parfait into a serving jar or other suitable vessel, such as a ramekin, to a level around 1 to 2cm from the top. Pour approximately half a teaspoon of melted butter over the top to seal. Alternatively, combine elderflower cordial with gelatine and leave to set, then chop, place in a piping bag with a small nozzle and pipe on top.

To make the salad

Mix the spices, seasoning and the flour and use the seasoned flour to coat the chicken livers. Pan-fry in a little oil until pink.

To make the relish

Place all of the ingredients in a thick-bottomed pan and boil for 1 hour until the liquid has reduced. Chill for one hour until set.

To serve, place the jar onto the plate with a good spoonful of relish alongside. Arrange a small handful of dressed salad leaves around the plate with the spiced livers on the top. Garnish with herbs and serve with a little toasted bread - the famous Poilâne rye bread is a perfect toast to go with it.

HAY-BAKED 'LOOSE BIRDS' CHICKEN WITH SWALEDALE-BAKED DAUPHINOISE, SMOKED SADDLEBACK BACON ROLLS AND BUTTERED SPINACH

HAY-BAKED 'LOOSE BIRDS' CHICKEN WITH SWALEDALE-BAKED DAUPHINOISE, SMOKED SADDLEBACK BACON ROLLS AND BUTTERED SPINACH

Main course - Serves four
Preparation time: 30 minutes
Cooking time: 1½ hours

1 large oven-ready chicken
200g hay
4 slices smoked bacon
200g spinach
a pinch of nutmeg
25g butter
seasoning

for the dauphinoise
6 baking potatoes
300ml whipping cream
1 clove garlic, finely chopped
1 sprig of thyme
20g butter, melted
100g Swaledale cheese
seasoning

Preheat the oven to 180°C/ gas mark 4. Season the whole chicken and wrap in the hay. Place in a roasting tray and place in the oven for approximately 1 hour 15 minutes.

Meanwhile prepare the dauphinoise potatoes. Peel the potatoes and slice thinly. Bring the cream to the boil and add the thyme and garlic. Layer the potatoes in an ovenproof dish, adding seasoning as you go. Pour over the cream, brush with the melted butter and grate the cheese on top. Bake for 45 minutes. Either serve in the cooking dish, or cut out 'rounds' with a pastry cutter. Keep warm.

To make the bacon rolls

Cut each bacon rasher into 3, roll up and hold in place with a cocktail stick. Bake for 10 minutes in the same oven.

Wilt the spinach in a frying pan with the butter, a little seasoning and the nutmeg.

Once the chicken is cooked, take to the table within the hay. Carve, serving with the bacon rolls, a stack of potatoes and spinach on the side.

A LITTLE BIT OF THEATRE FOR THIS LOCAL BIRD. IT'S GREAT AS A CENTERPIECE, BROUGHT TO THE TABLE SURROUNDED BY HAY, GARNISHED WITH THE BACON ROLLS, AND SERVED WITH A POT OF POTATOES AND SPINACH ON THE SIDE.

CHICKEN 'HOTCH POTCH' WITH STAR INN KITCHEN GARDEN VEGETABLES

Main course - Serves four
Preparation time: 45 minutes
Cooking time: 75 minutes

1 large, whole free-range chicken
500ml good chicken stock
1 glass fino sherry
2 star anise
8 baby carrots
1 clove of garlic, crushed
1 bulb of fennel
6 shallots, topped and tailed
2 bay leaves
5g flat parsley, chopped
25g broad beans
100g chilled butter, diced
a little oil for frying
seasoning

to garnish
a few garden herbs

to serve
crusty bread
dressed green salad leaves

Split the chicken down into breasts, legs and thighs, and liver, if you wish. Then, heat a little oil in a frying pan and seal all of the meat to a golden brown colour. Once cool, take a pad of kitchen towel and pat off all of the oil from the meat. Bring the chicken stock to the boil and add the sherry, bay leaves and star anise. Chop the fennel and carrots, then add to the stock, along with the chicken, shallots and garlic.

Simmer for 45 minutes until the chicken is cooked through. To finish, lift out the chicken and keep warm. Then rapidly reduce down the chicken stock by two thirds to form a broth-like 'juice' and add a few cubes of chilled butter. Spoon the chicken and the vegetables into a bowl or plate with a decent rim. Add the broad beans and parsley to the 'juices', simmer for two minutes, then check the seasoning and spoon over the meat and vegetables. Serve with crusty bread and a dressed green salad. Garnish with herbs and serve immediately.

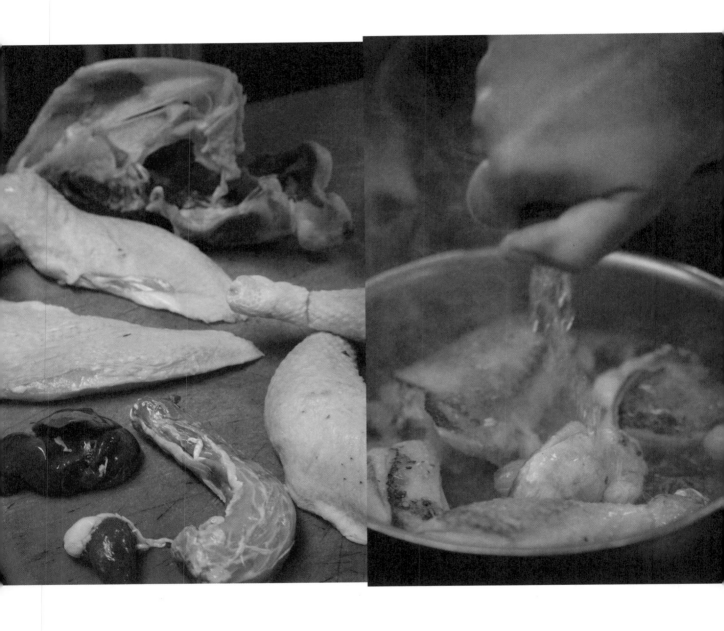

170_171

**CHICKEN 'HOTCH POTCH'
WITH STAR INN KITCHEN
GARDEN VEGETABLES**

A SOUPY SORT OF STEW IS THE BEST WAY, I THINK, TO
DESCRIBE THIS DISH. ALL THE PIECES — BREAST, THIGH,
DRUMSTICK, LIVERS — SERVED IN CONSOMMÉ-LIKE BROTH,
FULL OF THE BEAUTIFUL, FRESH FLAVOURS OF OUR KITCHEN
GARDEN — BEANS, BABY CARROTS, FENNEL, BAY LEAVES, ETC…
A 'HARVEST FESTIVAL' IN A POT!

'LOOSE BIRDS' CHICKEN, HAWES WENSLEYDALE AND HAMBLETON ALE PIE

'LOOSE BIRDS' CHICKEN, HAWES WENSLEYDALE AND HAMBLETON ALE PIE

Snack - Serves twelve
Preparation time: 1 hour
Cooking time: 1½ hours plus
standing and chilling time

for the hot water crust pastry
450g plain four
1tsp salt
200g lard
225ml milk and water,
   in equal proportions

for the pie filling
250g pork shoulder, minced
6 shallots, finely chopped
1 clove of garlic, crushed
6 chicken breasts, sliced into strips
100g Wensleydale cheese, cut
   into large 1cm thick slices
2 egg yolks to glaze
80g pickle of your choice
250ml Hambleton Ale
3 leaves of gelatine, previously
   soaked in water
seasoning

Preheat the oven to 160°C/
gas mark 3.

To make the pastry

First warm a mixing bowl and sift
the flour and salt into it. Make a
well in the centre. Heat the lard in
the milk and water in a saucepan
over a medium heat until just
reaching boiling point, then pour
into the well in the flour and stir
quickly with a wooden spoon
until thick. Continue working by
hand to form a smooth dough.
Cool slightly, then use the
dough to line a greased 20cm
tin, keeping some of the dough
for the lid separately in a warm
place. Put the tin onto a tray.

Mix the pork mince with the
shallot and garlic and season
to taste. Place a layer of the
pork mixture in the bottom of
the pie, then a layer of chicken,
then a layer of cheese and
a layer of pickle. Repeat the
layering until everything has
been incorporated and the pie
is full. Cut out the pie lid from
the remaining pastry, glaze the
edges of the pie and the lid with
the egg yolk, then place on the
lid and press down to seal.
Cut out a 1cm hole in the centre.
Glaze the pie lid and bake in
the oven for 50 minutes.
Once cooked, remove from
the oven and allow to stand
for at least 2 hours. Warm the
beer gently, squeeze the water
from the gelatine and add to
the warmed beer. The gelatine
should dissolve, giving the beer
a syrupy texture. Then, with a
jug or funnel, pour the beer into
the pie through the hole in the
lid. Chill in the fridge for 1 to 2
hours and use as required.

174_175

THESE ARE MORE OF A 'CUTTING' PIE OF THE PLOUGHMAN'S TYPE, IF YOU LIKE, GREAT FOR A BOXING DAY BUFFET OR A SUMMER'S DAY PICNIC – ANY EXCUSE, REALLY, THAT'S IF YOU NEED ONE.

BALLOTINE OF CORN-FED CHICKEN, YORK HAM AND FOIE GRAS, PICKLED BLACK TRUMPET MUSHROOMS, SAGE AND SHALLOT BRIOCHE AND YORKSHIRE RELISH

Starter - Serves six
Preparation time: 3 hours
Cooking time: 10 minutes

for the ballotine
1 large chicken
sufficient duck fat to cover
    the chicken
½ lobe duck/goose foie gras
75g York ham lardons,
    finely chopped
25ml brandy
25ml sherry
25ml veal jus
small handful tarragon,
    finely chopped
seasoning

for the Yorkshire relish
[make beforehand and store]
2 apples, roughly chopped
1 onion, roughly chopped
zest and juice of 2 oranges
2 tomatoes, roughly chopped
100g brown sugar
75ml white wine vinegar
5g ground mixed spice

for the pickled mushrooms
[can be made beforehand]
50g black trumpet mushrooms,
    cleaned
50ml white wine vinegar
25g sugar
1 star anise
1 clove
1 bay leaf

for the brioche
[can be made beforehand]
15g yeast
splash of milk, warmed to
    blood heat
1 tsp salt
250g strong flour
3 eggs plus 1 egg yolk with
    a little milk to glaze
170g butter
25g sugar
2 shallots, finely diced and
    sweated in a little oil
1 handful sage, finely chopped

To make the relish

Place all of the ingredients into a saucepan. Cook on a low heat for approximately one hour. Allow to cool, then blitz in a food processor until smooth. Use as required.

To make the pickled mushrooms

First place the vinegar, sugar, spices and bay leaf into a pan. Bring to the boil and allow to simmer for 5 minutes. Remove from the heat and add the mushrooms. Use as required.

Preheat the oven to 220°C/ gas mark 7.

To make the brioche

First crumble the yeast into the milk and stir until dissolved. Add the salt, flour and the 3 eggs and combine together. Knead the mixture until the mix is smooth and elastic. In a separate bowl, beat together the butter and sugar until very soft.

QUITE A PICTURESQUE DISH. THE PALE WHITENESS OF THE CHICKEN, PINK PIECES OF YORK HAM, RICH, BUTTERY FOIE GRAS AND THE FLECKS OF THE BLACK MUSHROOMS AROUND THEM. VERY RESTAURANTY INDEED.

Add this mixture to the dough a little at a time making sure each addition is thoroughly mixed in before adding the next. When combined, add the shallots and sage, then continue to beat for a further 15 minutes, until the dough has become smooth and shiny. Cover the bowl with a damp cloth and leave in a warm place (approximately 24°C) for about 2 hours. The dough should have risen and doubled in size. Knead the dough, turning it over quickly around three times. Cover again and refrigerate for several hours.

On a lightly floured surface, shape the dough into a large ball. Place into a greased and floured loaf tin. Glaze the top of the brioche with the egg yolk and milk glaze, brushing from the outside towards the centre. Retain the remaining glaze for a second application.

Leave to rise in a warm draught-free place for approximately one hour until the dough has almost doubled in size. Glaze the top of the brioche again and bake for around 40 minutes. Turn out of the tin immediately on removing from the oven.

Reduce the oven temperature to 120°C/gas mark 1.

To make the ballotine

First split the chicken into breasts and legs, retaining the remainder of the carcase for stock-making purposes. Place the breasts and legs in a deep oven tray and cover with the confit duck fat. Cover and place in the oven. After approximately 40 minutes, the breasts will be cooked. Remove these and return the legs to the oven for another hour, or so, until tender. Remove from the oven and set aside.

Next take the foie gras lobe and place in a deep oven tray with the brandy, sherry, jus and York ham. Place the tray in the oven for 5 to 10 minutes to render the fat from the foie gras. Allow to cool slightly and remove the veins from the centre with your fingers. Return the foie gras to the oven tray and leave to cool slightly.

Once the chicken legs are cool enough to handle, pick off all of the meat into bite-sized pieces and cut the chicken breasts and the foie gras into thin slices. Combine all of the meats together, add the York ham lardons and mix a little of the confit fat through it so as to bind the meats together. Season and add a little chopped tarragon.

Lay out three layers of cling film on top of each other and place the meat mixture evenly in a line along the nearest edge to you. Use the cling film to form the mixture into a firm 'sausage', approximately 2.5cm diameter. Tie at both ends and lay in a tray of iced water to cool the mixture without flattening the shape. When ready to use, slice with a serrated knife, serving 2 slices per portion, each about 1cm thick. Dot some Yorkshire relish around and add a few pickled trumpet mushrooms. Serve with the brioche.

176_177

DUE

CASTLE HOWARD.3PM

As the season moves on, so does the
climate, with the arrival of the dark,
dank days of autumn, and the sounds
of running becks and bubbling brooks.
The scent of snow is in the air, as
skeins of Canadian geese take up their
yearly ice-skating antics on Castle
Howard lake, after the flying formations
announce their arrival with a rousing,
endless chorus of rhythmic honking.

On the Bill

Wine Notes - Duck & Goose
by Andrew Firth

You have a lot to contend with here, with the fatty flavours and the richness of the meat. Andrew's dishes all have a traditional feel to them, a bit like a James Stewart film, so, maybe old-fashioned wines, good, weighty wines with acidity and tannins, are the order-of-the-day. Examples would be a Chateauneuf du Pape or Gigondas from the famous vineyards around Avignon, or the Rioja Reserva wines, which are aged in the barrel to give an oaky, vanilla tang. Heading off to Australia, you could try a Shiraz from Barossa or McLaren Vale, or for something completely different, maybe a Vouvray Sec from the Loire valley; a white wine with a touch of sweetness made from the Chenin Blanc grape.

UTH

DUCK & GOOSE: VERSATILE BIRDS, WILD OR FARMED, CRISPY AND JUICY, MUCH LOVED BY YOUNG AND OLD.

Michaelmas and Christmas are the most popular times of the year for goose consumption. Farm-reared geese are best, with greater consistency of flavour and taste. They should be hung for a few days to allow the meat to relax, and for the flavour to improve.

'Old' Canadian Geese look beautiful, but, aside from the show and splendour, they are basically as tough as old boots! Young Canadian Geese, such as greylags and 'pink feets' taste much better. They are, however, difficult to pluck and easy to overcook. It's best to use moist forcemeat with plenty of butter to keep the flesh succulent whilst cooking.

Duck is always a safe bet, everyone's friend. Crispy, roasted, confit and cooked pink, kids through to the oldies love it. It's always a winner. The Gressingham is widely available, it's slightly gamey, but still farmed, whereas the mallard is our main wildfowl.

Ducks arrive into our kitchen in early September. They are partnered with elderberries in a port and orange-infused 'Yorkshire Sauce', and make our Harome version of Duck à l'Orange. These slight birds need very little cooking, after normally being hung for 2-3 days.

We remove the breasts, for pan-frying for risottos and stir-fries, etc. But due to all their hard work paddling, their legs need to be slow-cooked, or, confit in fat to tenderise. You can tell the age of a bird by the colour of their bill; young birds' bills are brighter. Also, generally when you tear the web, the younger birds tear much easily.

Duck-shooting takes place at dusk and dawn generally, at lakes and ponds that are often man-made. The birds are shot when they come in to land, or when they prepare to take flight. This takes a lot of skill and organisation because of the limited time-frame and available light.

SO

PAN-ROAST BREAST OF 'LOOSE BIRDS' DUCK WITH SCRAMBLED

EGG, WILD GARLIC, CEP MUSHROOMS AND SWEET SHERRY GRAVY

Heat up a frying pan, season the duck breasts with salt and pepper, and place into the pan, skin side down. Dry-fry until the skin is crisp, then turn over and cook for approximately 4 to 5 minutes until pink. Lift out of the pan and leave to rest.

To make the gravy

First reduce the veal stock by half, then add the sherry and allow to continue to reduce to the required consistency.

Next, fry the mushrooms in melted butter and season.

To make the scrambled egg

Break the eggs into a bowl, add seasoning, a little cream and butter, and whisk. Warm a pan and heat the mixture, stirring constantly until the mix comes together. Fold in the chopped wild garlic.

Slice the duck and place on a warmed plate. Place the scrambled egg into an egg cup or alongside, if you so desire, sprinkle the fried wild garlic and mushrooms over the duck and finish off by pouring over the sauce. Serve immediately.

Main course - Serves four
Preparation time: 15 minutes
Cooking time: 15 minutes

4 duck breasts
4 duck eggs
100ml whipping cream
100g butter for the egg,
    and for frying
50g cep mushrooms
100g wild garlic leaves,
    finely chopped
20ml sweet sherry
200ml veal stock
seasoning

**PAN-ROAST BREAST OF 'LOOSE BIRDS'
DUCK WITH SCRAMBLED EGG, WILD GARLIC,
CEP MUSHROOMS AND SWEET SHERRY GRAVY**

THE LIGHTLY SCRAMBLED DUCK EGG, WITH CHOPPED WILD GARLIC FOLDED THROUGH THE DELICATELY COOKED EGGS, SPRINKLED WITH THE ODD FUNGUS COULD BE A MEAL IN ITSELF, FOR A VERY ROBUST BREAKFAST OR BRUNCH. AND WITH THE BREAST OF THE DUCK ADDED, IT IS STILL LIGHT, BUT FORMIDABLE. TRY IT!

HAROME HONEY-ROAST DUCK
'ON THE RÔTISSERIE' WITH
CINNAMON AND SPICES

188_189

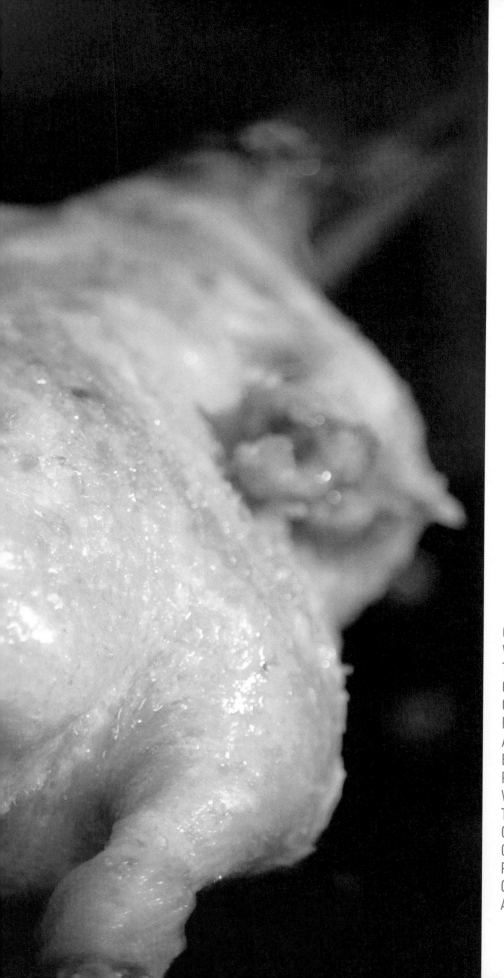

ON OUR 'CHEF'S TABLE',
WE HAVE A SMALLER KITCHEN
TO ENTERTAIN A GROUP OF
GUESTS WITH MORE OF A
ONE-ON-ONE RELATIONSHIP.
PART OF THE 'THEATRE' IS OUR
ALL-SINGING, ALL-DANCING,
BRASS AND DARK RED
RÔTISSERIE, WHICH COOKS
WHILST GENTLY BASTING.
THE FLAMES LICK THE SIDES
OF THE BIRD GIVING A LOVELY,
CRISP SKIN, AS IT SLOWLY
ROTATES, AND THE SPICES
GIVE OFF A COMFORTING,
ALMOST FESTIVE, AROMA.

HAROME HONEY-ROAST DUCK 'ON THE RÔTISSERIE' WITH CINNAMON AND SPICES

Main course - Serves four
Preparation time: 20 minutes
Cooking time: 1½ hours

2 whole, oven-ready ducks
1 orange
seasonal fruits, such as figs
2 cinnamon sticks
200ml clear, runny honey
10g cinnamon, ground
5g five spice or allspice, ground
seasoning

Preheat a rotisserie or oven to 160°C/ gas mark 3.

Prick the skin of the duck with a fork. Cut the orange in half and place both of these and the cinnamon sticks inside the cavity. Season.

Then warm the honey in a small pan until very runny, then mix in the ground cinnamon and five spice. Using a pastry brush, coat the duck skin all over. Place the ducks on the rotisserie spit or, if cooking in a normal oven, place in a roasting tray. Roast the birds for approximately 1½ hours to give a golden brown, crispy skin.

To serve, place the bird onto a suitable platter, dress with some watercress and take to the table whole. Take off the legs and carve into drumstick and thigh. Carve the meat from the breast into slices. Place the seasonal fruits into the roasting juice and warm through. Serve the juices and the fruits with the duck.

190_191

SOFT-BOILED REGGIE'S DUCK EGG WITH A TOASTED WHITE CRAB 'SANDWICH', NORTH SEA BROWN SHRIMP, BLADE MACE BUTTER AND CELERY SALT

Starter/Snack - Serves two
Preparation time: 10 minutes
Cooking time: 10 minutes

100g unsalted butter
5g mace blade, ground
50g brown shrimp, peeled
5g dill, chopped
2 slices brown bread
50g white crabmeat
zest of half a lime
10g cucumber, finely diced
2 tbsp mayonnaise
2 duck eggs
a sprinkling of celery salt
seasoning

to garnish
a few celery leaves

First make the crab sandwich, by adding the lime zest and cucumber to the crabmeat and binding together with the mayonnaise. Toast the bread and cut to rectangular shapes. Season the crab mixture to taste.

Add the mace blade and butter to a pan and clarify, add the shrimps at the last minute along with the dill.

Drop the duck eggs into boiling water and low to simmer for approximately 8 minutes. Remove from the water and serve with the sandwich, shrimp butter and celery salt. Garnish with celery leaves.

REG JOHNSON OF GOOSNARGH, THE 'DUCK MAN' [HIS FAME GOES GOES BEFORE HIM], IS ONE OF THE BEST SUPPLIERS OF POULTRY PRODUCTS IN THE COUNTRY. HIS DUCKS GRACE MANY A MICHELIN-STARRED TABLE AND WE USE THEM FROM TIME TO TIME, ALONG WITH THOSE FROM OUR 'LOOSE BIRDS' MAN, PAUL. THE EGGS FROM REGGIE ARE CONSISTENTLY GREAT. WE SOFT-BOIL THEM, MAKE LITTLE TOASTED SOLDIERS FOR DIPPING, AND SPOON OVER THE LITTLE PINK SHRIMPS. IT'S A VERY POPULAR DISH – NURSERY FOOD AT ITS BEST.

PAN-ROAST WILD DUCK WITH CITRUS FORCEMEAT, POACHED ELDER

BERRIES, SPICED CARROT PURÉE AND TRADITIONAL YORKSHIRE SAUCE

PAN-ROAST WILD DUCK WITH CITRUS FORCEMEAT, POACHED ELDERBERRIES, SPICED CARROT PURÉE AND TRADITIONAL YORKSHIRE SAUCE

Main course - Serves four
Preparation time: 30 minutes
Cooking time: 60 minutes

2 oven-ready wild ducks
50g butter
seasoning

for the forcemeat
200g pork sausagemeat
grated zest of ½ orange
grated zest of ½ lemon
4 shallots, finely chopped
50g soft breadcrumbs
1 egg
1 tsp sage, chopped
a little oil for frying
seasoning

for the purée
6 carrots
a little milk
2 tsp mixed spice
seasoning

for the Yorkshire sauce
200ml red wine
100g redcurrant jelly
zest of ½ orange
juice of one orange
75ml veal jus
a splash of rapeseed oil
75g elderberries

Preheat the oven to 180°C/ gas mark 4. Place the whole ducks in a roasting tray. Rub a little butter over the breast of the bird, season and roast for approximately 35-40 minutes.

To make the forcemeat

First fry the shallot in a little oil until soft, then add the grated rind of half of one lemon and one orange to the sausagemeat together with the chopped sage, breadcrumbs and beaten egg. Combine together, season to taste and place into a 25cm loaf tin. Cook in the oven for 30 minutes, then turn out.

To make the Yorkshire Sauce

Peel the remainder of the orange, remove the white pith and discard. Cut the zest into julienne strips and place in a saucepan with the red wine and redcurrant jelly. Juice the orange and add to the pan, reducing the liquid to a syrupy consistency.

To make the carrot purée

Peel and slice the carrots, then place in a pan with a little milk. Cook until very soft, then drain, season the carrots and blitz in a food processor to purée consistency. Finish with the mixed spice.

To serve, slice the duck breast onto the plate with the leg next to it and spoon on a little carrot purée. Drop the elderberries into the Yorkshire sauce and bring to the boil, then spoon over the wild duck. Serve immediately.

THE WILD DUCK OR MALLARD IS IN ABUNDANCE IN EARLY SEPTEMBER, A VERY MUCH-LIKED, MIDDLE-GROUND GAME BIRD WHICH IS NOT TOO STRONG IN FLAVOUR. BUNCHES OF ELDERBERRIES FROM HEAVY-HANGING ROADSIDE BUSHES AND THE CITRUS UNDERTONES OF THE FORCEMEAT AND THE YORKSHIRE SAUCE, GIVE SIMILAR FLAVOURS TO THE SEVENTIES CLASSIC 'DUCK À L'ORANGE'.

TRADITIONAL MICHAELMAS GOOSE WITH ALL THE TRIMMINGS

'EAT A GOOSE ON MICHAELMAS DAY, WANT NOT FOR MONEY ALL YEAR!'

IT WAS ALWAYS THOUGHT THAT EATING GOOSE ON 29TH SEPTEMBER, THE FEAST OF ST MICHAEL, WOULD BRING YOU GOOD FORTUNE FOR THE REST OF THE YEAR. GREEN GEESE, FED IN THE FIELDS, WERE USED RATHER THAN THE FATTER CHRISTMAS BIRD, AND ARE TRADITIONALLY GARNISHED WITH APPLES, DUE TO THE AMOUNT OF WINDFALLS AROUND AT THIS TIME OF YEAR.

Main course - Serves four
Preparation time: 45 minutes
Cooking time: 3 hours

for the goose
1 x 4-5kg goose
2 tsp runny honey
1 tsp mixed allspice
seasoning

for the bread sauce
4 slices of bread, white
    and crushed
a good pinch of mixed
    ground spice
1 white onion shredded
    with fresh whole cloves
400ml milk
seasoning

for the apples
4 small eating apples
a little allspice
a little unsalted butter

for the forcemeat
150g sausagemeat
50g unsalted butter
1 egg yolk
30g breadcrumbs
1 tsp garden sage, chopped
50g onion, finely diced
grated zest of half an orange

for the gravy
50ml cider
250ml chicken stock
seasoning

to garnish
1 pinch watercress

Preheat the oven to 190°C/
gas mark 5.

To prepare the goose

First prick the skin gently all over
with a fork or the tip of a sharp
knife. Cover with a little runny
honey and sprinkle over the
allspice and seasoning, then place
on a cooking rack or trivet in a
deep roasting tray (as the amount
of fat that comes out of the meat
is amazing: beware!) Place in the
oven allowing 20 to 25 minutes
per $\frac{1}{2}$kg plus an extra 20 minutes
to make sure, so around $2\frac{1}{2}$ to 3
hours in total. When cooked, take
care when removing from the
oven due to the amount of fat –
it's worth taking care of as it
makes wonderful roast potatoes.
You can even rub it on your chest
or use it to keep your harnesses
and saddlery supple!

Cut the tops off a third of the way
down the apples, sprinkle with
a little allspice, add a smidge of
unsalted butter, and then replace
the tops. Combine all of the
forcemeat ingredients together,
then form into 4cm balls, slightly
flattened on each end. Place
the apples and forcemeat balls
together on a non-stick baking
tray and cook in the oven for
approximately 10 minutes or until
cooked through. Keep warm.

To make the bread sauce

First add the onion to the milk and
bring to the boil. Let this infuse for
approximately 20 minutes, then
remove the onion and the cloves.
Add the breadcrumbs, spice and
seasoning. Cook gently to a loose,
dropping consistency. Set aside
and keep warm.

Pour off the fat and remove the
bird from the tray. Keep the bird
warm and add the cider and stock
to the residue in the roasting
tray. Bring to the boil and reduce,
skimming off the excess fat.
When the required consistency for a
thin gravy is achieved, pass through
a sieve, season and keep warm.

To serve, lift the lids from the
apples, place a forcemeat ball
on top, then replace the lid.
Arrange around the goose and
tuck a little watercress into the
bird for garnish. Carve at the table.

**TRADITIONAL MICHAELMAS
GOOSE WITH ALL THE
TRIMMINGS**

BEDALE FARM.4.20PM

When we were kids, my brother, for some unknown reason, decided to keep 'skinny bods' (as they used to be known down the Esk Valley), or 'middle-of-the-road birds', as Mr Firth now calls them. I think he had a multi-million pound money-making scheme planned out, but their popularity wasn't massive thirty years ago, as it isn't now really. The demand was low and the feed costs were high, costing him more than he could charge for the birds. Added to that, when it came to the crunch, he couldn't kill them either. Poor Dad (our resident chief executioner!) had to 'do' them for him.

GUINEA FOWL: BECOMING EVER-PRESENT, AND MORE POPULAR. OFFERING A GREAT GAME OPTION IN THE SUMMER MONTHS. REARED FOR THE TABLE, SO THEY MAKE A GREAT MEAL, WITH THE TEXTURE OF CHICKEN, AND A STRONG, EARTHY, GAMEY FLAVOUR.

Birds of a Feather

Wine Notes - Guinea Fowl
by Andrew Firth

The guinea fowl is sort of the chicken of game birds, with middle-of-the-road flavours, but it isn't served so often, so should have its own wine-match ideas. We are looking for medium-bodied wines, as Andrew's dishes have a sort of fruity, ripe theme running through them, so I think the wines should as well, such as Cabernet/Merlot from Australia or New Zealand, or a Stellenbosch Cabernet Sauvignon. Alternatively, try a Cru Bourgeois Claret from the Médoc, or we can go back to Burgundy and get a good Bourgogne Rouge from a fancy producer. Pinot Noir from Chile, with all its fruity flavours, would also be good and for Lil's white wine selection, a Rosé from Tavel or, perhaps, a Cabernet Rosé from the new world.

Together

They would screech, sometimes in the middle of the night, especially if Charlie Fox was on the prowl. They roosted in a shed, just behind our farmhouse, at the top of some mossy stone steps. They lived a cosy life, with a wire-run to let them spread their wings, which is more than the mass-produced Continental imports, filling most of our supermarket and butchers' shelves have. The French love the bird, probably due to their lack of proper game (in France, it isn't an official game bird unless you are off shooting it in a jungle somewhere in a far-off land!).

Normally corn-fed, guinea fowl offer something different during the summer months. They are reared for the table rather than for sport and shooting. They put on a good show with their full plumage, but when naked, they have a 'skinny' appearance because of their high breast bone and wide, rather than deep, breast meat. When they are handled properly, and paired with a suitable garnish, they make a great meal. They are becoming increasingly popular and more widely available from farms in this country. Maybe my brother was partly responsible for the 'skinny bod' movement - just ahead of the times!

Flock

A LIGHT LUNCHTIME DISH FOR
SUMMER. THE DELICATE TASTE
OF GUINEA FOWL GENTLY
COOKED WITH THE 'UMPH'
OF LEMON BALM WHICH
GROWS PROLIFICALLY IN OUR
GARDENS AND A LITTLE SHAKE
OF MOREL MUSHROOMS IN A
SPLODGE OF GARLIC BUTTER
TASTES MAGIC!

BREAST OF CORN-FED GUINEA FOWL WITH GARDEN LEMON BALM RISOTTO, MOREL MUSHROOMS AND CRISPY YOADWATH MILL KILN-SMOKED HAM

Main course - Serves two
Preparation time: 30 minutes
Cooking time: 20 minutes

2 corn-fed guinea fowl breasts
a little rapeseed oil

for the risotto
1 shallot, finely chopped
1 clove of garlic, crushed
200g risotto rice
500ml chicken stock
50ml white wine
20ml double cream
1 bunch lemon balm
25g hard cheese, grated. Such
    as Parmesan or Doddington's,
50g bacon lardons, cooked
100g morel mushrooms, dried,
    if fresh are unavailable
150ml chicken stock,
    already reduced
a pinch of tarragon, chopped
20g unsalted butter, chilled
2 slices of crispy Yoadwath Mill
    kiln-smoked or Parma ham

Preheat the oven to 180°C/
gas mark 4.

Place the guinea fowl breasts
onto a roasting tray, season and
brush with a little oil. Roast for
12 minutes, then allow to rest,
whilst keeping warm.

To make the risotto

Fry off the chopped shallot and
crushed garlic in a saucepan,
add the risotto rice and white
wine stirring continuously
whilst the stock is added bit
by bit, until cooked 'al dente'.
Finish with chopped lemon
balm, the grated cheese, cream
and the bacon lardons..

Crisp the ham under a grill for
a couple of minutes. Heat the
chicken stock, then add a knob
of chilled butter, a pinch of
chopped tarragon and the
morel mushrooms.

Place the risotto in the centre
of the plate, or in a separate
vessel, slice the guinea fowl
breast in two and place on top
of the risotto, then finish with
the crispy ham and the morel
mushroom 'gravy'.

210_211

BREAST OF CORN-FED GUINEA FOWL WITH GARDEN LEMON BALM RISOTTO, MOREL MUSHROOMS AND CRISPY YOADWATH MILL KILN-SMOKED HAM

CORN-FED GUINEA FOWL BREAST 'CAESAR-STYLE'

Starter/Snack - Serves four
Preparation time: 20 minutes

2 guinea fowl breasts,
    cooked and sliced
3 small baby gem lettuces
50g white bread, diced
10ml olive oil
seasoning

for the dressing
100ml mayonnaise
25g Coolea cheese, grated
1 clove garlic, crushed
25g anchovies in oil, drained

to garnish
75g Coolea cheese shavings
25g anchovies in oil, drained
a few garden herbs
4 slices pancetta, cooked

First make the Caesar dressing, by placing the mayonnaise in a food processor with 25g of grated cheese, the garlic and 25g anchovies. Blend until smooth.

Wash the baby gems, pick off the leaves and allow to dry on a kitchen towel.

Place the bread and pancetta on a preheated baking tray and drizzle with the oil. Season and bake at 160°C/gas mark 3 for approximately 5 minutes, until crispy.

To assemble the salad, first place the baby gem leaves, with the sliced fowl breasts and croutons in a bowl. Gently mix in the dressing, until all of the leaves are coated. place into a serving dish and finish with the remaining anchovies and shavings of coolea, the pancetta sices and a few garden herbs.

THIS CLASSIC SALAD USES THE MARINATED SPANISH-STYLE ANCHOVIES IN SUNFLOWER OIL, AS OPPOSED TO THE SALTED VARIETY, WITH SHAVINGS OF COOLEA CHEESE, A GOUDA-TYPE MADE BY A DUTCHMAN IN IRELAND, BLENDED WITH THE DRESSED BABY GEM LETTUCE AND PLUMP PIECES OF GUINEA FOWL. PERFECT AS LITTLE CANAPÉS, WHICH WE SERVE IN BAMBOO CONES AT WEDDINGS AND PARTIES.

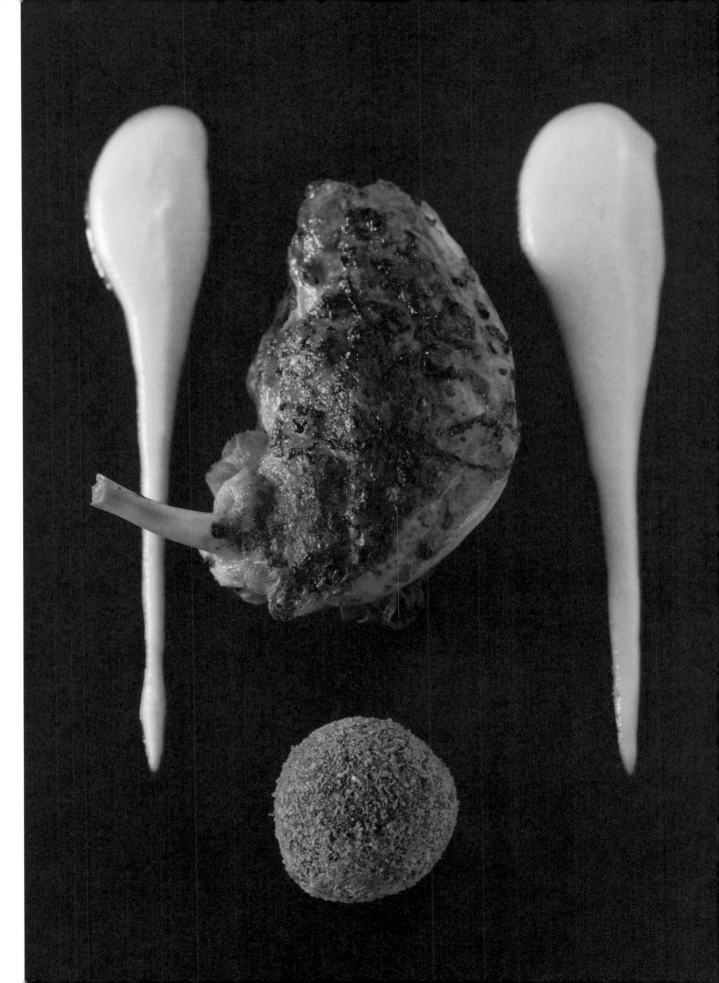

PAN-FRIED BREAST OF CORN-FED GUINEA FOWL WITH A BLACK PUDDING SCOTCH EGG, PURÉE OF JERUSALEM ARTICHOKE AND ROASTED MIRABELLE PLUM JUICES.

214_215

PAN-FRIED BREAST OF CORN-FED GUINEA FOWL WITH A BLACK PUDDING SCOTCH EGG, PURÉE OF JERUSALEM ARTICHOKE AND ROASTED MIRABELLE PLUM JUICES.

Main course - Serves four
Preparation time: 45 minutes
Cooking time: 25 minutes

4 guinea fowl breasts
a little rapeseed oil

for the scotch eggs
150g black pudding
75g sausagemeat
4 quails' eggs
2 eggs and a little milk
150g fresh breadcrumbs
50g flour
a little oil for frying
seasoning

for the purée
200g Jerusalem artichokes
200ml milk
10g butter
seasoning

for the plums
6 mirabelle plums
150ml reduced beef stock
a knob of unsalted butter
1 tbsp redcurrant jelly

First make the scotch eggs, by blending together the black pudding, sausagemeat and a little seasoning. Cook the quails' eggs for 2 minutes in boiling water, then drain and refresh in iced water. Once cooled, peel off the egg shells, then encase the cooked eggs in the black pudding mix, forming small balls. Whisk the eggs in a bowl with a little milk to make an egg wash, place flour in a second bowl and breadcrumbs in a third. Dip the scotch eggs, in turn, in the flour, then the egg, then the breadcrumbs. Deep-fry the eggs at 180°C for 4 minutes.

To make the Jerusalem artichoke purée, first peel the artichokes, then chop and place in a saucepan with milk, butter and seasoning. Bring to the boil and cook until soft, then drain off the milk. Blend the artichokes in a food processor until smooth and purée consistency.

For the plum juices, peel and de-stone the plums. Boil in the stock until the plums break down, and the liquid has reduced. Add the redcurrant jelly and stir in a little butter.

Pan-fry the guinea fowl breasts until golden brown and set aside to rest. To serve, spoon a little of the artichoke purée onto each plate, and place a black pudding scotch egg on top. Slice the breast onto the plate. Serve the plum sauce separately.

WE MAKE THE SCOTCH EGGS USING BLACK PUDDING TRIMMINGS WITH A LITTLE SAUSAGEMEAT TO BIND IT TOGETHER, WHICH IS THEN MOULDED AROUND A SOFT-BOILED QUAIL EGG AND BREAD-CRUMBED. THEY ARE GREAT AS SNACKS IN THEIR OWN RIGHT. THE MIRABELLE PLUMS HAVE A SHORT SEASON AROUND THE END OF AUGUST/BEGINNING OF SEPTEMBER. WE LIGHTLY CARAMELISE HALVES OF EACH OF THE PLUMS FOR PRESENTATION PURPOSES AND TO COUNTERBALANCE THE SLIGHT ACIDITY OF THE FRUIT.

TAGLIATELLE OF CORN-FED GUINEA FOWL WITH SUMMER VEGETABLES, LOWNA DAIRY GOATS' CHEESE AND A SALAD OF BALDERSBY HERITAGE TOMATOES

PASTA, GUINEA FOWL AND VEGETABLES — THIS IS
ONE WAY OF GETTING THE KIDS TO EAT DECENT FOOD!
LOVELY MEAT, PEAS, BROAD BEANS, ASPARAGUS AND
A CREAMY SAUCE MADE WITH THE MILD LOWNA DAIRY
GOATS' CHEESE FROM THE EAST YORKSHIRE WOLDS,
SERVED WITH A SIDE SALAD OF MIXED HERITAGE
TOMATOES, SUCH AS GREEN GRAPE, WHITE BEAUTY
AND RED BRANDY WINE.

TAGLIATELLE OF CORN-FED GUINEA FOWL WITH SUMMER VEGETABLES, LOWNA DAIRY GOATS' CHEESE AND A SALAD OF BALDERSBY HERITAGE TOMATOES

Starter - Serves four
Preparation time: 45 minutes
Cooking time: 10 minutes

for the tagliatelle
2 breasts of corn-fed guinea fowl
200g fresh pasta tagliatelle,
    made from basic pasta dough
    recipe as below
75g Lowna Dairy goats' cheese
4 asparagus spears
50g garden peas
50g broad beans
100ml cream
100ml dry white wine
a little oil
seasoning

for the salad
4 heritage tomatoes
50ml olive oil
1 banana shallot, sliced
fresh basil, roughly chopped
    at the last minute
cracked black pepper

to garnish
garden herbs
baby tomatoes, lightly-fried

basic pasta dough
[makes 450g of dough]
300g Italian "00" pasta flour
3 large fresh eggs
a generous pinch of salt

Cut the guinea fowl breasts into strips and season. Heat up a frying pan, and fry the breast meat in a little oil, add the broad beans, peas and asparagus spears and cook for a further 2 minutes, then add the white wine and reduce by half. Finally, add the cream and goats' cheese to make a light sauce.

Meanwhile, add a little oil and salt to a pan of water and bring to the boil. Add the pasta and cook for 2 minutes, until al dente. Drain well and add to the sauce. Combine gently, then spoon into deep bowls. Garnish with garden herbs and some lightly-fried baby tomatoes. Serve immediately with the salad of sliced tomatoes and shallots dressed with olive oil and seasoned with cracked black pepper and basil.

For the pasta dough

Mix ingredients together thoroughly with a wooden spoon, knead with your hands – use a little more flour, if required. The dough should be smooth and elastic after around 10 minutes. Rest for 15 minutes, then roll and cut using a pasta machine or hand-cut with a large chopping knife.

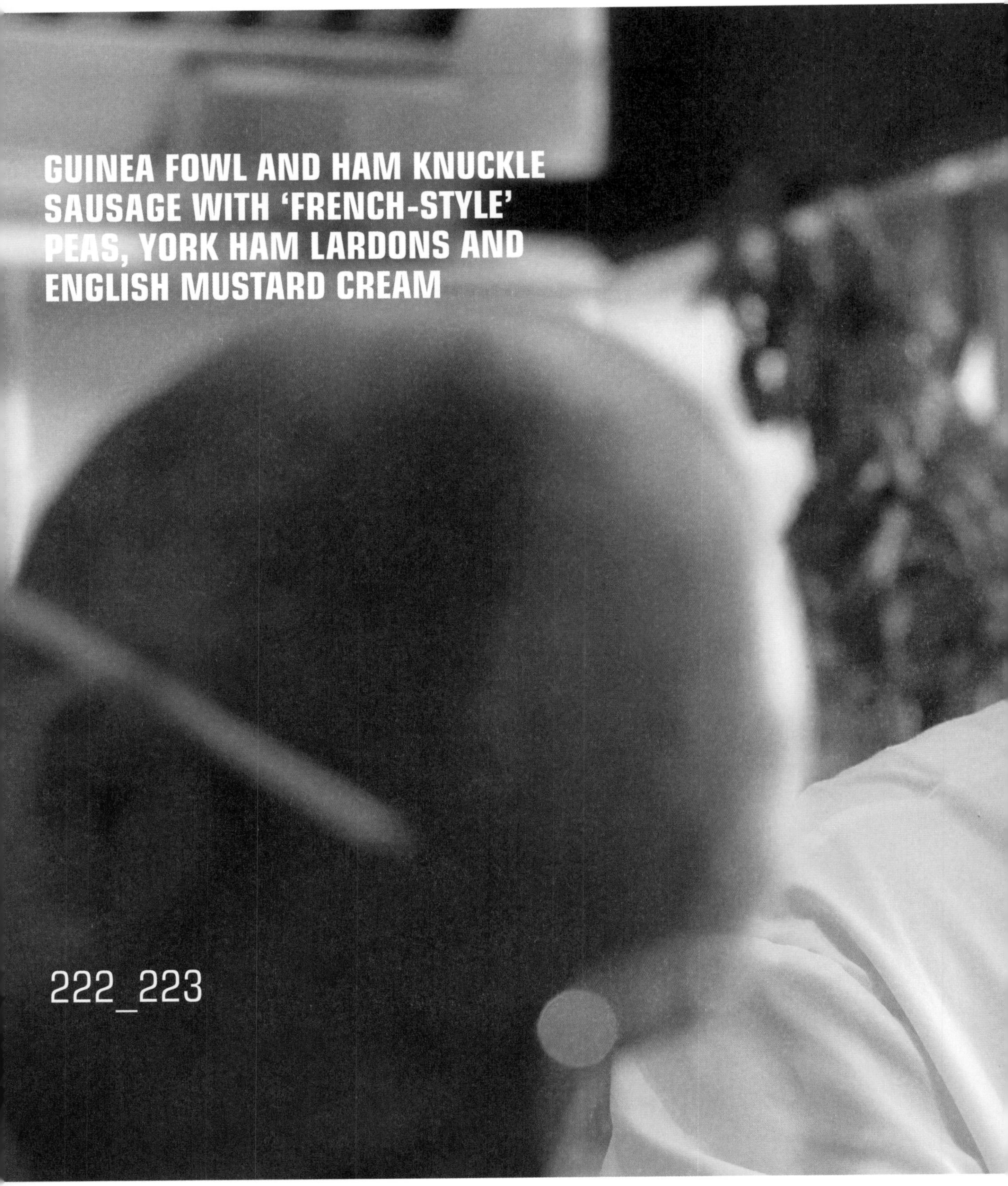

GUINEA FOWL AND HAM KNUCKLE
SAUSAGE WITH 'FRENCH-STYLE'
PEAS, YORK HAM LARDONS AND
ENGLISH MUSTARD CREAM

THIS IS LIKE THE CONTINENTAL STYLE 'BOUDIN BLANC', MORE OF A MOUSSE-TYPE SAUSAGE WITH FLECKS OF HAM THROUGH IT AND SOME SPICY GREEN PEPPERCORNS. THE FRENCH-STYLE PEAS GO VERY WELL ALTHOUGH, UNFORTUNATELY, THE DIET WILL TAKE A BIT OF A BASHING, BUT WHAT THE HELL; THAT'S WHY IT TASTES SO GOOD!

Main course - Serves four
Preparation time: 2½ hours
Cooking time: 30 minutes plus
4½ hours for the ham knuckle

for the sausages
2 guinea fowl breasts
250g ham knuckle, cooked and
    chopped into ½ cm dice
aromats, such as carrot, leek,
    onion, bay leaves and black
    peppercorns
10ml whipping cream
50g soft butter
1 egg
50g fresh breadcrumbs

for the peas
200g peas, fresh or frozen
50g lettuce, such as little gem,
    cos or iceberg, sliced thinly
50ml whipping cream
80g York ham lardons
20g shallots, peeled and sliced
    into rings
5g mint, chopped
seasoning

for the sauce
10ml white wine
90ml whipping cream
2 tsp English mustard
seasoning

to garnish
fresh herbs or pea shoots

GUINEA FOWL AND HAM KNUCKLE SAUSAGE WITH 'FRENCH-STYLE' PEAS, YORK HAM LARDONS AND ENGLISH MUSTARD CREAM

Soak the ham knuckles overnight, wash off, then place into a boiling pan with some aromats: use washed and chopped carrot, celery, leek, onion and bay leaves. Cover with cold water and add a few black peppercorns, then bring to the boil and simmer for $3\frac{1}{2}$ to 4 hours. Alternatively, purchase a good quality cooked ham and use as recipe; there is no major difference when cooking on a small scale, and it's somewhat quicker! When cool, chop the ham into $\frac{1}{2}$ cm dice.

Skin the guinea fowl breast and dice the meat, then pureé in a food processor with the egg, breadcrumbs, butter and 10ml of cream. Add the ham knuckle meat to the pureé and season. Place into a piping bag and chill for 1 hour, then pipe the mixture to form plump 'sausages' approximately 10cm long, on a triple layer of cling film to form a 'skin'. Tie a knot at one end and twist the other end to seal (see also recipe for Pan-roast Roe Deer Saddle with Homemade Juniper Sausage, Wensleydale-creamed Cavolo Nero, Baked Greengage 'Tatin', Stones Green Ginger Wine Juices on pages 74_77 for a more detailed explanation of the process). Chill the sausages for 30 to 45 minutes, then gently pan-fry them to colour all sides. Keep warm.

To make the French-style peas, place the peas, lettuce, 50ml of the cream, the shallots and lardons into a saucepan and boil until the cream has reduced. Add the mint and season. Keep warm.

For the sauce, reduce the white wine, then add the remaining cream and the English mustard. Season to taste. Keep warm.

To plate the dish, first place a large spoonful of the french-style peas onto the plate, or in a suitable vessel, with the guinea fowl sausage next to it. Drizzle the mustard cream around the plate and garnish with some fresh herbs or pea shoots, if available. Serve immediately.

KITCHEN GARDEN.MIDNIGHT

A stone's throw from the kitchen, our garden provides us with an endless supply of scents and flavours, and is scattered with an incredible array of edible flowers, loved by humans and animals alike.

Breeding Ground

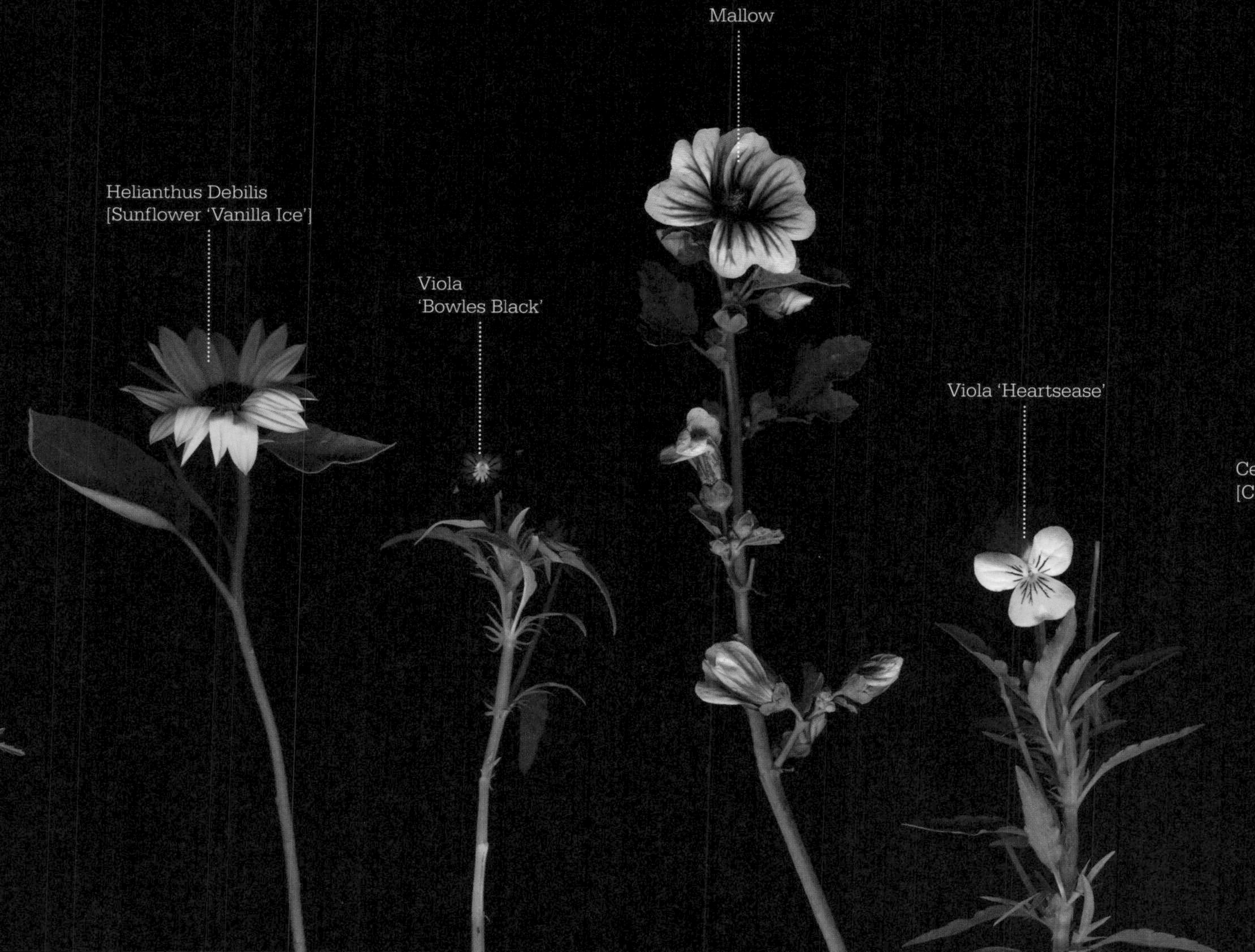
Mallow
Helianthus Debilis [Sunflower 'Vanilla Ice']
Viola 'Bowles Black'
Viola 'Heartsease'

Never recently top of the popularity polls in this country, the hare is probably more popular than the poor old rabbit, although the latter makes for a decent, cheap and healthy stew, a casserole, or of course, the good old 'rabbit pie'. How could we forget that?

RABBIT & HARE: HEALTHY MEAT, HIGH IN PROTEIN AND LOW IN FAT. IN SOME PEOPLES' EYES, IT'S UNFORTUNATELY SEEN AS A CASE OF 'FUR COAT AND NO KNICKERS!' THE HARE IS A BIG CHARACTER, SURROUNDED BY MYTH AND MYSTIQUE, MUCH-RESPECTED BY COUNTRY-TYPES. IT'S FULL OF FLAVOUR WITH PLENTY OF TASTE.

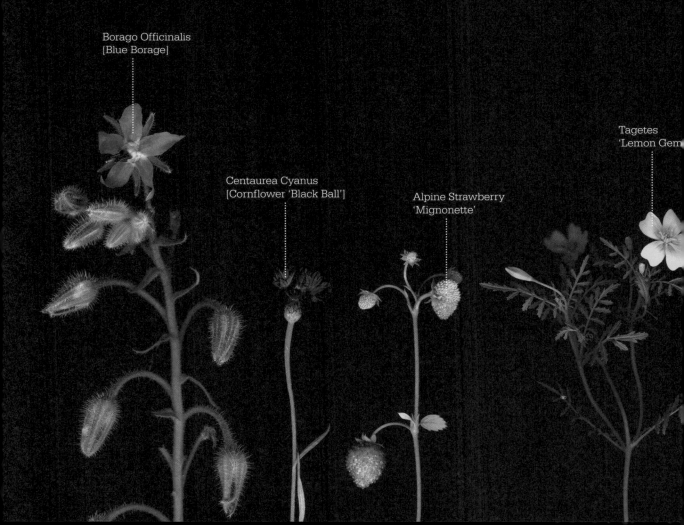

Borago Officinalis
[Blue Borage]

Centaurea Cyanus
[Cornflower 'Black Ball']

Alpine Strawberry
'Mignonette'

Tagetes
'Lemon Gem

Bright Eyes

Wine Notes - Rabbit & Hare
by Andrew Firth

What about a pint of really good beer, just for a change?

The meat of the hare is quite different to rabbit and, obviously, the dishes vary. I think, go 'country' with a Minervois, Corbières or similar from Languedoc, or one of the great reds from southern Italy, such as a Salice Salentino from Puglia, or from Navarra in Spain. Navarra is situated just next door to Rioja and uses the same grapes and techniques, but the wines are 33% cheaper. New world thoughts go to Chile and South Africa, and, perhaps, a Syrah...

To do this yourself, take off its feet at the first joint, slice a bit of the skin and fur, then pull the skin over the saddle and the forelegs. There will be a lot of blood inside the rib cage, so be aware, and be ready to collect the goodness for later use. Keep all the usual bits (heart, lungs, kidney and liver) for terrines, garnish, faggots, etc. Mmmm... game faggots!

Meanwhile, back with the bunnies... Over the years, many places have become ridden with these 'not so' furry friends. In Victorian times, the 'Rabbit Train' ran each week from the country to Smithfield Market. Leadenhall Street would have thousands neatly hanging, cleaned and pink-fleshed (My dad always says I looked like a skinned rabbit when I was born. That doesn't say much for rabbits, I'm afraid!). As rabbits breed like rabbits, they became a great source of cheap and healthy meat, widely available. Since then, popularity and demand has declined somewhat.

After World War II, myxomatosis was introduced into the country, spreading rapidly through the rabbit population, thus reducing their out-of-control numbers. It blinded and deafened the poor creatures, leading them to waste away and eventually die. The sight of animals on many British roads, staring into your headlights, hardly built up an appetite – think, bright eyes burning like fire! Thankfully, this is now in the past, and cheap, less glamorous meats and cuts have become fashionable again, thanks to the London boys.

Calendula Officianalis
[variety unknown]

Centaurea Cyanus
[Red Cornflower]

Nasturtium
'Tom Thumb'

Tagetes
'Golden Gem'

The hare has been somewhat elevated by the restaurant trade, and has become one of the best sellers on the menu. We give it the all-star treatment, as 'Royale', or 'Rossini', adding truffles, foie gras, etc. It has the air of superiority, the top drawer of the game world. Think jugged hare, thickened with its own blood, richer than richness itself!

'The Mad March Hare' is true to a certain extent, as they tend to breed in March, and the flavour of the meat changes for the worse! The hare has been associated with gazing at the moon, and various fables. Druids wouldn't eat it. Romans lived in fear of it. Hares are certainly a formidable sight as they bound across the stubble and arable fields. They are a good size, and often up to half a stone in weight.

One afternoon in late winter, some local lads bagged thirty three within a couple of hours. I've never seen so many hares in one place, still warm and almost alive. Like most things, the younger the hares, the better! Hares improve for eating after being hung, head-down, for about a week or so in the cooler winter months (less if the days are getting milder and warmer). Add a splash of vinegar to the blood to stop it coagulating, and place it in a fridge, ready to be 'jugged', when the hare has been skinned, by basically peeling off its furry jumper.

Garlic Chive Flower

Lavender 'Hidcote'

Calendula Officianalis 'Indian Prince'

Red Clover

ynas 'Blue Boy']

Tropaeolum Majus [Nasturtium 'Black Velvet']

BRAISED MUSCOATES WILD RABBIT WITH HOME-GROWN GLOBE ARTICHOKES, BABY CARROTS AND FENNEL, PICKERING WATERCRESS PURÉE, ROASTED FRESH ALMONDS AND VERBENA JUICES

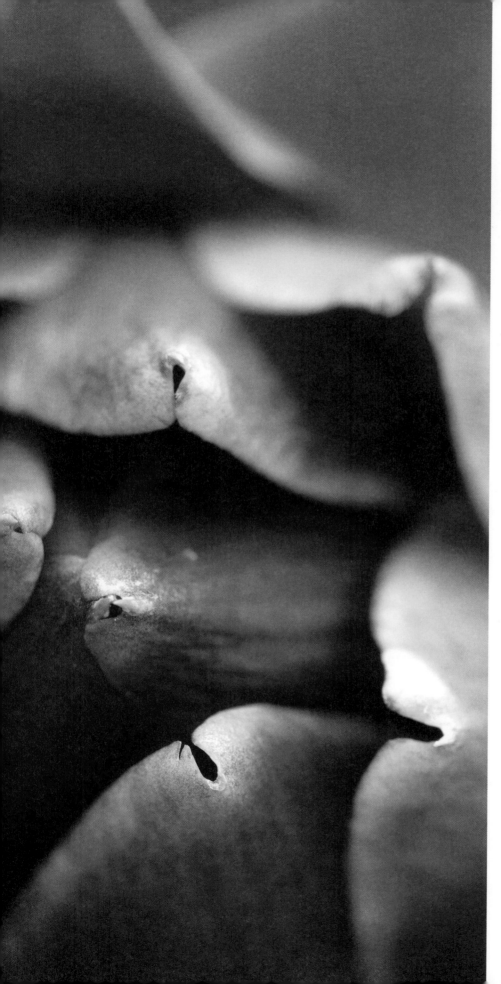

ADRIAN DANGAR, WHO SUPPLIES US WITH WILD RABBITS, LIVES AT MUSCOATES GRANGE, A COUPLE OF MILES AWAY FROM THE PUB. I'VE KNOWN HIM MOST OF MY LIFE, AS HIS FATHER LIVED ON A FARM NEAR TO US ALONG THE ESK VALLEY, WHEN I WAS A CHILD. HE IS VERY MUCH A COUNTRY SPORTSMAN, HUNTING, SHOOTING AND FISHING. THE LOVELY SWEET GAMINESS OF THE BRAISING RABBIT FILLS THE KITCHEN WITH A MOUTH-WATERING AROMA. THE REST OF THE INGREDIENTS ARE STRAIGHT OFF PETER RABBIT'S SHOPPING LIST!

Main course - Serves four
Preparation time: 1 hour
Cooking time: 3 hours

1 whole wild rabbit, skinned
    and jointed
750ml chicken stock
mirepoix vegetables [onion,
    celery, bayleaf, garlic,
    peppercorns]
2 globe artichokes
juice of one lemon
4 baby carrots
2 baby fennel
50g unsalted butter, warmed
15g whole fresh almonds, peeled
seasoning

for the purée
2 bunches of watercress
250g chicken stock [use from
    rabbit cooking liquor]
seasoning

for the sauce
50g lemon verbena stalks
    and leaves
a little chilled butter

to garnish
a few edible flowers or
    garden herbs

Preheat the oven to 140°C/ gas mark 1. To prepare the rabbit, first remove the front and back legs, then cut the saddle in half. Braise the legs and saddle in 750ml chicken stock with the mirepox vegetables for 2½ hours.

For the watercress purée, blanche the two bunches of watercress in boiling salted water for one minute, then refresh in ice cold water. Blend with a little chicken stock and season with salt and white pepper. Set aside.

Warm the almonds in a pan. Blanch the carrots and fennel, then refresh as for the watercress. Check the rabbit is cooked, then lift out and drain. Rapidly reduce down the rabbit cooking liquor to make the sauce. Add the lemon verbena and check the seasoning. Keep warm. Cook the globe artichoke in lemon juice and water. Place the carrots and fennel in warmed butter and season. Next place the rabbit onto a hot plate.

Spoon the hot buttered vegetables around, add a little chilled butter to the reduced stock and check the seasoning. Pass through a sieve over the rabbit and serve immediately with a shot of the watercress pureé and a few garden herbs for garnish.

BRAISED MUSCOATES WILD RABBIT WITH HOME-GROWN
GLOBE ARTICHOKES, BABY CARROTS AND FENNEL,
PICKERING WATERCRESS PURÉE, ROASTED FRESH
ALMONDS AND VERBENA JUICES

THE INSPIRATION FOR THIS CAME FROM MARCO PIERRE
WHITE'S 'WHITE HEAT' COOKBOOK, THE FEUILLETÉ OF
RABBIT HE DESCRIBES AS BASICALLY A POSH RABBIT PIE!
WE GARNISH IT WITH SEASONAL HERBS AND VEGETABLES,
AND A FEW SLIVERS OF BLACK TRUFFLE, ALTHOUGH THIS IS
PURELY INDULGENCE AND NOT BY ANY MEANS COMPULSORY.

POSH MUSCOATES WILD RABBIT PIE WITH DODDINGTON'S CHEESE SHAVINGS, BLACK TRUFFLE AND SHERRY CREAM

POSH MUSCOATES WILD RABBIT PIE WITH DODDINGTON'S CHEESE SHAVINGS, BLACK TRUFFLE AND SHERRY CREAM

Main course - Serves four
Preparation time: 1 hour
Cooking time: 2 hours

2 whole, medium-sized
    rabbits, jointed
20ml oil for frying
1 clove of garlic, peeled
    and crushed
1 onion, peeled and roughly
    chopped
2 sticks of celery, washed and
    roughly diced
1 leek, washed, trimmed and
    roughly chopped
2 carrots, washed, peeled and
    roughly diced
50ml sherry
300ml chicken stock
250g puff pastry
1 egg yolk
50ml milk
100ml cream
1 tsp grain mustard
4 tsp parsley, chopped
150g Doddington's cheese
    shavings
20g black truffle shavings
    [optional]
seasoning

to serve
garden herbs

Preheat the oven to 200°C/
gas mark 6.

Heat the oil in an ovenproof pan,
season the rabbit pieces with salt
and pepper, and add to the pan,
browning on all sides. Add the
crushed garlic, the onion, celery,
leek and carrots and colour lightly.
Then add the sherry and allow
to reduce by half, then add the
chicken stock, cover and place
into the oven for approximately
1½ hours, until tender.

Roll out the puff pastry to a
thickness of 5mm, then cut
out four 10cm diameter shapes
using a round cutter, if available.
Score another round shape with
a diameter of approximately
8cm onto the centre of each
'round' making sure not to cut
all of the way through the pastry.
Criss-cross the top of the pastry
rounds with the back of a knife.

Position on a baking tray,
then mix together the egg yolk
and milk and brush the egg
wash over the pastry rounds.
Place the tray into the oven for
around 10 minutes until golden
brown. Then remove from the
oven and allow to cool on a rack.
Once cooled, cut out the central
disc with a small knife to form
a lid. Keep warm.

Lift the rabbit pieces from the
stock, and 'pick' large pieces of
meat from the bone. Keep warm.
Reduce down the cooking liquor,
then add the cream and reduce
by half to a coating consistency,
add the grain mustard and check
the seasoning. Return the rabbit
pieces and add the parsley to
the sauce, and bring to the boil.

Place the pastry rounds onto
a warmed plate, then fill each
pastry with one portion of the
rabbit. Position the lid on top
and spoon a little sauce around.
Garnish with the cheese and
truffle shavings, and a few
garden herbs.

HAROME-SHOT HARE 'ROSSINI'

Main course - Serves two
Preparation time: 30 minutes
Cooking time: 20 minutes

a little oil for frying
loins from 1 hare saddle
2 rashers smoked bacon
2 x 10cm round bread croutons
50g game pâté [or use the offal
    from the hare, fry off and blend
    to a paste]
splash of Madeira wine
200ml reduced game stock
20g yellow chanterelles or other
    wild mushrooms
2 x 50g pieces of foie gras
seasoning

to finish
a drizzle of white truffle oil
a few shavings of fresh truffle

Lightly oil a frying pan and place on a medium heat. Season the hare loins and pan-fry for approximately 4 minutes, then allow to rest and keep warm. Fry the smoked bacon at the same time for flavour, then lightly fry the croutons in the same pan (to soak up the juices), until golden brown.

Once the croutons are cooked, spread the pâté onto the top and slice the hare loin onto this, with the crispy bacon.

Finally, deglaze the pan with the Madeira, add the reduced stock and the mushrooms, and allow to simmer for approximately 2 minutes.

Pan-fry the foie gras in a hot pan, season lightly and drain. Finally, place the foie gras on top of the hare and spoon the hot sauce over. Finish with a drizzle of white truffle oil and fresh truffle, if available.

GIOACCHINO ROSSINI, THE ITALIAN COMPOSER, WAS A GREAT LOVER OF THE NICER THINGS IN LIFE SUCH AS FOIE GRAS AND TRUFFLES, INGREDIENTS WHICH APPEAR IN MOST DISHES BEARING HIS NAME. HERE, WE USE A LOIN FROM THE SADDLE, COOKED FOR ONLY 1 TO 2 MINUTES EACH SIDE, SO THAT IT IS FAIRLY RARE. THEN WE PLACE THIS ON A 'PÂTÉ' CROUTON TO ABSORB ALL OF THE JUICES, LIKE A SPONGE!

BRAISED
RABBIT SADDLE,
BROAD BEAN
AND BACON
RISOTTO, GRILLED
BOUDIN NOIR
AND GARDEN
LOVAGE JUICES

I KNOW BRAISING IN SUMMER
SEEMS UNNECESSARY BUT,
IN THE RESTAURANT TRADE,
PRE-COOKED FOOD CUTS
CORNERS AND, BY BEING
CLEVER, WE HAVE A QUICK
AND RELATIVELY EASY DISH TO
SERVE AS GAME, WHEN THERE
IS A SHORTAGE OF FEATHERED
GAME. WE COMBINE WITH
SHELLED BROAD BEANS AND
PAR-COOKED RISOTTO - ALL OF
THE FLAVOURS COMPLEMENT
EACH OTHER FANTASTICALLY.

BRAISED RABBIT SADDLE, BROAD BEAN AND BACON RISOTTO, GRILLED BOUDIN NOIR AND GARDEN LOVAGE JUICES

Starter - Serves four
Preparation time: 20 minutes
Cooking time: 1½ hours

for the rabbit
a little oil for frying
4 rabbit saddles
2 litres chicken stock
1 onion, chopped
2 carrots, roughly chopped
1 clove of garlic, crushed
   and chopped
2 sprigs of thyme
10 lovage leaves,
   roughly chopped

for the risotto
50g shallots, peeled and diced
a little rapeseed oil for cooking
200g risotto rice
500ml chicken stock
50g broad beans, peeled
100g smoked bacon lardons
75ml whipping cream
50g cheddar cheese, grated.
seasoning

4 x 50g pieces of boudin noir
   or black pudding

for garnish
4 strips of smoked streaky
   bacon, cooked
fresh herbs

In a large, heavy-bottomed pan, colour the saddles of rabbit in a little oil, add the chicken stock and bring to the simmer, add the onion, carrot, garlic and thyme to the stock, and cover with a lid or some foil. Cook gently over a low heat for approximately one hour. Then remove the saddles and keep warm. Pass the stock through a strainer and discard the vegetables. Return the stock to the heat and reduce rapidly to a light 'sauce' consistency. Add around 10 chopped lovage leaves and leave to infuse. Keep warm.

To make the risotto, first sweat the shallot in a drop of rapeseed oil in a heavy-bottomed pan without colouring only for 1 to 2 minutes, add the rice, stir briefly again, add 500ml chicken stock, a ladle at a time, cook out the rice, stirring all the time, so it doesn't stick and until most of the stock has evaporated. Add the broad beans and lardons, the cream and the cheese, then check the consistency and seasoning. The rice should be 'al dente' (firm to the bite).

Heat up the grill and cook the boudin noir for approximately 4 minutes.

To finish, take the rabbit saddles and remove a loin from each side. Place into the sauce to warm though. Place a little risotto onto each plate or bowl with two loins on each, and a slice of the grilled boudin noir on top of each portion. Finish with the lovage juices and some smoked bacon and garden herbs, such as chive flowers. Serve immediately.

**HAROME-SHOT HARE HOT POT
WITH BAKED PAN HAGGERTY**

246_247

A WINTER WARMER, IF EVER I'VE KNOWN ONE, SIMMERING HARE STEW, RICH IN COLOUR AND FLAVOUR, WITH ROOT VEGETABLES SOAKING UP THE JUICES, AND PIECES OF SMOKED BACON, RED WINE AND AROMATIC HERBS ALL ADDING A 'BURGUNDY'-FEEL TO THE OCCASION. THE 'PAN HAGGERTY', A TRADITIONAL NORTHUMBERLAND BAKED POTATO, ONION AND CHEESE DISH, BRINGS IT DOWN TO EARTH. IT'S VERY, VERY MOREISH!

HAROME-SHOT HARE HOT POT
WITH BAKED PAN HAGGERTY

Main course - Serves four
Preparation time: 1½ hours
Cooking time: 2 hours

for the hare hot pot
1 medium/large hare, skinned
 and jointed
a little oil for frying
10g plain flour
200g piece of smoked bacon,
 cut into 2cm dice
500g large, mixed root vegetable
 [such as swede, parsnip, carrot
 and celeriac], diced
150g baby onions, peeled
5 sprigs of thyme
2 bay leaves
6 juniper berries, crushed
2 cloves of garlic, peeled and
 roughly chopped
1 bottle of 'decent' red
 cooking wine
500ml game stock
seasoning

for the pan haggerty
1 onion, sliced
50ml rapeseed oil
600g mixed root vegetables,
 such as celeriac, carrot and
 potato, grated
75g mature Wensleydale
 cheese, grated
50g unsalted butter
5g garden thyme, chopped
seasoning

Preheat the oven to 180°C/
gas mark 4.

For the pan haggerty

First sweat the onion, cooking
gently in the butter and oil
until soft. Pat dry the grated
vegetables with a tea towel
to absorb as much of the
moisture as possible. In a
small ovenproof dish, layer the
vegetables alternatively with
the grated cheese and a little
thyme, seasoning each layer and
finishing with cheese. Place the
dish into the oven for 45 minutes
to 1 hour, until cooked through.
Finish under a hot grill for a
gratinated, crispy finish.
Use as required.

For the hare

Take a thick-bottomed pan and
heat a little oil. Flour and season
the hare pieces and fry off with
the bacon, gently to colour to a
golden brown. Increase the heat
after 3 to 4 minutes and add all
of the root vegetables, the baby
onions, garlic, juniper berries and
herbs, stirring all of the time. Add
the red wine and stock and cook
on a low heat for around 1½ to 2
hours until tender. When cooked,
lift out the meat and reduce
the cooking liquor to a syrupy
consistency. Check the seasoning
and pour back over the meat.

Place the hare onto a warm
plate with a wedge or stack of the
pan haggerty served alongside.

We are never far from some good
fishing in Harome, as the rivers Rye
and Riccal flow very near the village,
towards Nunnington and Ness.
Take a walk down past The Pheasant,
and follow the rise over the old iron
bridge, past Sim Barker's, and further
on, past the old railway station, and
there you'll find the meandering river,
running swiftly, like a babbling brook,
but with a deceptively strong current
in certain parts. It's as much a spot
for picnicking families in summer as
for eager fishermen, but it's also
popular with cormorants and herons.
The re-stocking of the river works
well in replenishing the stomachs
of greedy Mr Heron and his mates!

TROUT & WILD SALMON:
A CYNIC ONCE REMARKED
'SALMON FISHING IS LIKE A
BLIND MAN ON A DARK NIGHT,
SEEKING A BLACK CAT IN A
SHUTTERED ROOM, WHEN
THE CAT ISN'T EVEN THERE!!'

RIVER ESK.LUNCHTIME

Wet´n Wild

256_259

BALLOTINE OF RIVER ESK WILD SEA TROUT WITH CAPER AND CUCUMBER KETCHUP, 'SALAD' OF HOMEGROWN HERBS AND HERITAGE POTATO, AND BROWN SHRIMP FRITTERS

260_263

POACHED SANDSEND-LANDED WILD SALMON WITH SOFT-BOILED 'MOLLET' HENS' EGG, RAINBOW CHARD SALAD AND LEMON BALM MAYONNAISE

264_265

HOME-SMOKED RIVER ESK SALMON WITH TOASTED CRUMPET, PEPPERED GARDEN SPINACH, POACHED VILLAGE DUCK EGG AND BUCKLER SORREL HOLLANDAISE

266_269

CONFIT OF WILD SALMON WITH GARDEN 'FRENCH' SORREL VELOUTÉ AND ROAST RIVER DOVE CRAYFISH TAILS

270_273

WARM SEA TROUT MOUSSE WITH A PURÉE OF PICKERING WATERCRESS, SHALLOW-FRIED SMOKED EEL AND HORSERADISH 'CROQUETTES', AND MUSTARD CRESS

Wine Notes -
Trout & Wild Salmon
by Andrew Firth

Chardonnay, a quality white Burgundy, is delicious - or a fine new world Chardonnay – with these. Trout sometimes has more flavour and the Esk Sea Trout dish needs richer wine, more new world Chardonnay, than the Sandsend Salmon, which would be lovely with a Maçon Blanc. You can go red with these, to keep Uncle Ted happy – a Pinot Noir goes well, as does a Fleurie or something similar, nothing too tannic and dry, really.

Further upstream, the setting is more serene, in the shade of the shallow gravel beds where the aerated conditions are ideal for their eggs to grow. The water is clean, oxygen-rich and cool. In the early spring, a few weeks after they hatch, the new-born 'alevin' move downstream to feed and forage for themselves. Because the food in our rivers is limited, the fish have to swim further afield to have their fill. After about three years, they are known as 'smolt', and will be about 20-30 centimetres in length, and at this point, they enter the 'Big, Wide, and Wonderful', heading out of the estuary into the great North Sea. This would be daunting enough in a full-sized fishing vessel, let alone for a puny little 'poisson', but their diet calls for bravery as they go it alone to hopefully dine on a smorgasbord of prawns, crabs, eels and other Scandinavian specialities. The dangers in the sea are immense, and the mortality rate is high, with only one in a hundred fish surviving.

This transition, from quiet, homely, freshwater tranquillity to the saline world of the open sea, puts the salmon in the premier league of 'anadramous' fish, capable of living in both types of water and able to swim in either direction.

UP

Having spent a couple of years or so in the North Norwegian Sea, eating their fill and getting up to full weight, they are then ready by some bizarre irony to repeat their epic journey in reverse, heading all the way back to my grandfather's stretch of river, as if the first journey wasn't enough! Back they swim to the exact place where they first hatched, past familiar obstacles, wildlife, fishing lines and nets, locks, weirs and dams. At Sleights, however, by my mum and dad's land, there is a manufactured 'ladder' to make life slightly easier at the last hurdle!

With climatic changes, a lack of rain often leaves river levels low, especially in spring and summer when they make their return journey. Just for good measure, they stop eating when they re-enter freshwater, and eventually their flesh and muscle tissue is eaten away from the inside, and they start to become weak. Add to this the various battle scars, lice and whatever else the elements have thrown at them, and they are probably not in the best fettle, but still they continue on their arduous journey. This fish really does know how to work for its supper. Its lifestyle creates a beautiful healthy fish, that tastes so much better than its flabby, luminous, farmed cousin.

STREAM

The slightly more 'grown-up' version of fishing is very close to home, more through memory than location. My grandfather used to have fishing rights on the River Esk whilst living in the lovely old house of Esk Hall, situated two or three miles upstream from the famous old port of Whitby, my birthplace. I remember the rods, and the landing nets, the waders, and, most plainly, the fish. As with any fisherman, the size of the catch tended to vary with the story, and the audience, and the tipple! Many more fish were caught in those days, as various things have changed, but thankfully the 'Wind in the Willows' setting has always remained the same. Standing, looking upstream from the dam, on a lazy, hazy late spring Sunday afternoon, the river would appear still, with rays of sunshine dancing on the surface, and insects dodging the mouths of the hungry salmon. Then, suddenly, rings of water would begin to ripple outwards, just before the roar of the salmon leap, where gallons of fresh, rust-red water (the colour of Yorkshire Tea), trickled down from the Moors, gathering momentum, to rush over the ladder which salmon 'climb' to spawn their eggs.

Those we use are mainly brown or sea trout, prepared and cooked simply. A poached ballotine, a fillet, or a darne, served with our own garden produce, whether it's podded peas or bursting broad beans, together with some minted and buttered Jersey Royals, and a dollop of lovage hollandaise, can't often be beaten in early summer. I remember the trout Guy Stephenson caught and brought to us one summer's evening, as a gift for the lads and lasses in the kitchen. It was prepped and eaten within the hour. The food of the Gods, and so, so simple. Staff meals ain't bad at The Star!

BALLOTINE OF RIVER ESK WILD SEA TROUT WITH CAPER AND CUCUMBER KETCHUP, 'SALAD' OF HOMEGROWN HERBS AND HERITAGE POTATO, AND BROWN SHRIMP FRITTERS

POACHED SEA TROUT WITH CAPERS AND SHRIMPS, TOPPED WITH A LITTLE FLAVOURED CRÈME FRAÎCHE, IS PERFECT WHEN YOU ARE SITTING IN THE GARDEN WITH A GLASS OF CHABLIS, ENJOYING THE LAST OF THE SUMMER SUNSHINE. IT'S A GREAT DISH FOR LARGE PARTIES, AS THE TWO FILLETS ARE 'STUCK' TOGETHER AND POACHED, THEN SLICED THROUGH TO GIVE A NICE, ROUND CIRCLE, WHICH MAKES FOR GREAT PRESENTATION.

Starter - Serves four
Preparation time: 20 minutes
Cooking time: 10 minutes

for the ballotine
2 x 200g sea trout fillets,
    skinned but pin-boned
2 leaves of gelatine, soaked
50g mixed chopped herbs
seasoning

for the potato salad
250g new potatoes
10g mixed herbs, chopped
4 tbsp crème fraîche
zest of one lemon
seasoning

for the ketchup
½ cucumber, skinned and
    de-seeded
40g capers
1 tsp dill, chopped
4 tbsp homemade or good
    quality proprietary
    mayonnaise
seasoning

for the fritters
60ml milk
60g unsalted butter
150g plain flour
2 egg yolks
100g brown shrimp, peeled
oil for deep-frying

to garnish
fresh garden herbs
a few cooked brown shrimp
optional: a little soured cream
    and caviar

To make the ballotine

Place the trout fillets, head-to-tail, next to each other, skinned side on a tray and season. Soak the gelatine leaves in a little cold water until soft, then lay over one of the trout fillets, and place the other trout fillet on top, so that both are still head to tail. Roll the combined fillets in the chopped herbs, then wrap in cling film, twisting the ends to make a sausage-like shape. Poach in boiling water for 15 minutes, remove from the water, then chill in fridge overnight.

To make the potato salad

Cook the new potatoes in boiling, salted water for approximately 10 minutes. Once cooked, drain and allow to cool. When cool, cut the potatoes into 2cm dice and mix in the chopped herbs, crème fraîche, a little lemon zest and seasoning.

To make the ketchup

Place the cucumber and capers into a food processor and blitz to a purée. Add the dill, season and mix in mayonnaise to a ketchup consistency.

For the fritters, first bring the milk to the boil, add the butter and allow to melt, then add the flour and mix to a thick paste. Continue mixing until the paste cools, then add the egg yolks and beat until the mixture leaves the sides of the pan. Add the shrimps and combine into the mixture. Chill for 1 hour, then roll into small balls approximately ½cm in diameter. Deep-fry the fritters for 2 minutes at 180°C, until golden brown. Drain and keep warm.

To serve, first cut the ballotine into 4cm slices with a sharp knife, allowing one slice per person. Place some potato salad in the centre of each plate with a slice of the ballotine on top. Dot the ketchup around the edge of the plate and arrange 2 to 3 fritters per person on each plate. Garnish with fresh herbs and a few shrimp. If you are feeling flamboyant, a little soured cream and caviar never goes amiss!

BALLOTINE OF RIVER ESK WILD SEA TROUT WITH CAPER AND CUCUMBER KETCHUP, 'SALAD' OF HOMEGROWN HERBS AND HERITAGE POTATO, AND BROWN SHRIMP FRITTERS

POACHED
SANDSEND-
LANDED WILD
SALMON WITH
SOFT-BOILED
'MOLLET'
HENS' EGG,
RAINBOW CHARD
SALAD AND
LEMON BALM
MAYONNAISE

BILL, OUR WILD SALMON MAN, HAS THE ENTHUSIASM OF A MAN POSSESSED. WITH A ZZ TOP BEARD AND CLAD IN SHORTS AND SANDALS, HE BOUNDS INTO THE KITCHEN. HAVING HAD AN EXTREMELY GOOD JOB ABROAD, HE DECIDED TO GO FOR THE 'EASIER' LIFE, CATCHING SALMON, SEA TROUT, LOBSTER AND CRABS OFF THE WHITBY COAST. THE FISH ARE JUST HOURS OLD WHEN WE RECEIVE THEM — YOU CAN'T GET BETTER SERVICE THAN THAT.

262_263

POACHED SANDSEND-LANDED WILD SALMON WITH SOFT-BOILED 'MOLLET' HENS' EGG, RAINBOW CHARD SALAD AND LEMON BALM MAYONNAISE

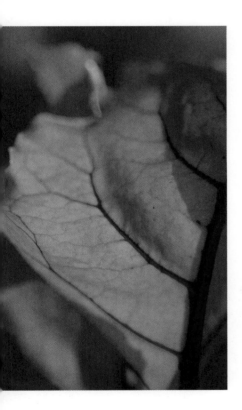

Main course - Serves four
Preparation time: 30 minutes
Cooking time: 20 minutes

for the salmon
4 x 150g wild salmon steak fillets
1 bay leaf
6 black peppercorns
juice of 1 lemon
seasoning

for the mayonnaise
2 egg yolks
1 tsp Dijon mustard
100ml virgin olive oil
1 tsp white wine vinegar
1 bunch of lemon balm, chopped
seasoning

4 hens' eggs
50g unsalted butter
1 bunch of rainbow chard
seasoning

to garnish
a few garden herbs
a little finely chopped shallot

Bring a pan of water to the simmer and add the juice of the lemon, the bay leaf and the peppercorns. Season the salmon fillets and cook in the simmering water for around 6 minutes. Once cooked, remove from the cooking water and drain on kitchen towel.

Cut the stalks from the chard, and wilt both stalks and leaves in a hot frying pan. Season and keep warm.

Boil the eggs for 5 minutes, then cool in iced water. Remove the shells and set aside.

To make the mayonnaise

Put the egg yolks, with the mustard and vinegar into a mixing bowl and whisk together. Then, slowly add the oil until the mixture is thick. Finish with the lemon balm. Check seasoning and set aside.

To serve, place the salmon in the centre of the plate with the chard stalks. Spoon the lemon balm mayonnaise into a piping bag and pipe or spoon large 'dots' of mayonnaise around the plate. Add the egg, first removing the top, if you wish garnish with the chard leaves, a little sliced shallot and a few garden herbs.

HOME-SMOKED RIVER ESK
SALMON WITH TOASTED
CRUMPET, PEPPERED GARDEN
SPINACH, POACHED VILLAGE
DUCK EGG AND BUCKLER
SORREL HOLLANDAISE

THIS WOULD SORT YOU
OUT FOR BREAKFAST;
IT'S BASICALLY 'OEUFS
FLORENTINE' WITH A TWIST.
IT WOULD BE GREAT ON
CHRISTMAS DAY MORNING,
ADDING TO THE OCCASION
AND SETTING YOU UP FOR
THE REST OF THE FESTIVITIES.
[MERRY CHRISTMAS!!]

Starter/Snack - Serves four
Preparation time: 30 minutes
Cooking time: 20 minutes

4 good slices of oak-smoked
    salmon
4 duck eggs
a little white wine vinegar
200g spinach leaf
a little butter
a pinch of nutmeg
cracked black pepper

for the hollandaise
2 hen egg yolks
50ml white wine vinegar
1 shallot, sliced
1 bay leaf
2-3 peppercorns
250g unsalted clarified butter
50g buckler sorrel, finely chopped

for the crumpets
150g strong white flour
10g fresh yeast
5g sugar
4g salt
100ml water, hand hot
    (approximately 37°)
150g butter

To make the crumpets

Mix together the flour, yeast,
sugar, salt and water in a mixing
bowl. Cover and leave to prove in
a warm place for 30 minutes, by
which time you should be able
to see bubbles starting to form
on top of the mixture. Heat some
small frying pans or crumpet/
pastry rings on a low heat and
add a knob of butter to each one.
When melted, spoon in a couple
of tablespoons of mixture
and allow it to cook slowly.
Small holes should begin to
form on the top of the crumpet,
after around 4 minutes. Finish in
a low oven (140°C/gas mark 2)
for a further 3 to 4 minutes and
turn out.

Poach the duck eggs in simmering
water, with a little white wine
vinegar added, for approximately
2 minutes, so that the centres are
still soft.

To make the hollandaise

First add the sliced shallot,
peppercorn and bay leaf to the
white wine vinegar, then reduce
until only a tablespoon remains.
Remove the aromats. Place the
egg yolks into a mixing bowl
and add the vinegar reduction.
Cook the mixture lightly over a
bain-marie, gradually adding and
whisking in the melted, clarified
butter, until very thick. Season
to taste. Mix the chopped sorrel
into the sauce.

Wilt down the spinach in a pan
with a knob butter, and season
with black pepper and a good
pinch of nutmeg.

Toast a crumpet under a warm
grill, remove and place in the
centre of the plate. Place a slice
of smoked salmon on top, with
a layer of spinach on top of this.
Gently place the poached egg
on top of the spinach and spoon
over the hollandaise sauce.
Serve immediately.

CONFIT OF WILD SALMON WITH GARDEN 'FRENCH' SORREL VELOUTÉ AND ROAST RIVER DOVE CRAYFISH TAILS

266_267

Fishing with the 'Cray twins' [AKA Tilly and Louis] in the river, just down from the village duck pond. Alas, to no avail on this occasion! Its a good job we have a reliable fishmonger on call.

A 'CLASSIC'. THE ACIDITY
OF THE FRESH SORREL
CUTS THROUGH THE SLIGHT
FATTINESS OF THE SALMON
— THE RICH TASTE OF
WILD SALMON IS FAR, FAR
SUPERIOR TO THE FARMED
VERSION, AND CRAYFISH TAILS
ARE FAIRLY EASILY AVAILABLE,
ALTHOUGH SCALLOPS OR
LANGOUSTINE TAILS CAN
ALSO BE SUBSTITUTED.

Main course - Serves four
Preparation time: 30 minutes
Cooking time: 30 minutes

4 x 150-200g supreme of
    wild salmon
250ml rapeseed oil
4 sprigs of thyme
4 cloves of garlic, peeled
2 star anise
6 black peppercorns
12 baby onions

for the velouté
125ml vermouth
500ml fish stock
300ml whipping cream
white pepper and salt
400g sorrel, finely diced
12 crayfish tails, lightly cooked

to garnish
a few garden herbs

In a shallow-sided pan or tray,
warm the oil and add the
baby onions, along with the
thyme, garlic, star anise and
peppercorns to 110°C, then
add the salmon supremes and
poach for 10 to 12 minutes.

Whilst these are cooking, heat
up a saucepan, then pour in
the vermouth and fish stock,
and reduce by a half. Add the
cream and reduce down again
to a coating consistency.
Check seasoning and keep warm.

Remove the salmon from the
tray and place on some kitchen
paper to drain. Keep warm.

Heat up the sauce and drop in
the crayfish and chopped sorrel.
Spoon onto warmed plates,
with the crayfish at triangular
points, and place the salmon
in the centre. Peel back half of
the salmon skin and garnish
with a few of the aromats
and some garden herbs.
Serve immediately.

**CONFIT OF WILD SALMON WITH GARDEN 'FRENCH'
SORREL VELOUTÉ AND ROAST RIVER DOVE CRAYFISH TAILS**

WARM SEA TROUT MOUSSE WITH A PURÉE OF PICKERING WATERCRESS, SHALLOW-FRIED SMOKED EEL AND HORSERADISH 'CROQUETTES', AND MUSTARD CRESS

270_271

A BIT OF A CHEF'S DISH,
THIS ONE. THE 'QUENELLES',
AS WE CHEFS LIKE TO CALL
THEM, ARE SPOON-MOULDED,
OVAL-SHAPED PORTIONS OF
TROUT MOUSSE POACHED
IN STOCK, SERVED WITH A
VIBRANT, PEPPERY PURÉE OF
PICKERING WATERCRESS, AND
A LITTLE 'STONEHENGE' SET
OF SMOKED EEL CROQUETTES
SITTING ON THEIR TAILS,
SPRINKLED WITH MINI FRILLS
OF MUSTARD CRESS.

WARM SEA TROUT MOUSSE WITH A PURÉE OF PICKERING WATERCRESS, SHALLOW-FRIED SMOKED EEL AND HORSERADISH 'CROQUETTES', AND MUSTARD CRESS

Starter - Serves four
Preparation time: 1½ hours
Cooking time: 45 minutes

for the mousse
200g sea trout fillets, skinned
    and boned
75ml cream
2 egg whites
a little butter
zest of 1 lime
white pepper and salt
a few aromats, such as
    star anise, etc

for the croquettes
50g smoked eel fillet
1 tsp horseradish, finely grated
200g mashed potato
1 egg and a little milk
50g flour
100g fresh breadcrumbs
rapeseed oil for frying
seasoning

for the purée
2 bunches of watercress
50g unsalted butter
a splash of cream, approx 10ml
seasoning

to garnish
1 small pinch of mustard cress
a few peashoots

Preheat the oven to 110°C/ gas mark ½ . Place the sea trout fillets, 75ml of cream, a little lime zest and 2 egg whites to a food processor and blitz to a fine pureé, check seasoning, then chill the pureé for one hour.

Next make the croquettes, first mix the smoked eel and horseradish into the cold, mashed potato and season. Take small handfuls of the mixture and roll into small 2cm by 1cm sausage shapes, then chill. Whisk one egg with a little milk, in a small bowl, and place the flour and breadcrumbs into 2 more bowls. Dip the chilled potato mixture first in the flour, then in the egg, then in the breadcrumbs, to coat completely. Heat a little oil in a frying pan, and fry the croquettes until golden brown. Keep warm.

Poach the sea trout mousse by simmering a little seasoned water with a few flavourings (star anise, etc) and forming 'quenelles' with two tablespoons, spooning inside each other to form an oval rugby ball shape or put the mixture into a piping bag and piping 5cm lengths instead. Then cook these for 4 to 5 minutes in the water with a little buttered greaseproof paper to cover and ensure even cooking. Once cooked, remove from the liquid and drain on kitchen towel.

To make the watercress pureé

First wilt the watercress stalks and leaves in a little unsalted butter. Add a splash of cream. Blitz to a purée and season.

To plate, warm the croquettes and quenelles of sea trout through in the oven for 3 to 4 minutes. Place a spoonful of warm watercress purée in the centre of a warmed plate, with the croquettes at alternative 'thirds' on top of the purée and the quenelles in between. Garnish with a little mustard cress and a few peashoots. Serve immediately.

Through

A couple of salads come into this section. The 'Salade Pérnigourdine' is a throw-back to my college days. It's a lovely, luxurious, light dish with a few treats added, as is the lobster 'Niçoise' with quail eggs, which can in fact be replaced with soft-boiled pheasant or duck eggs, and often is at The Star, depending on availability. Both salads are perfect for a summer's lunch, as a starter, or a main course. Hopefully, they demonstrate my fresh approach to using game, aiming towards lighter alternatives with colour and good flavour, keeping away from the traditional winter stodge that is sometimes associated with it.

Once the clocks have gone back, it's a time when the wet, clumpy mud of winter sticks to your boots, unless there has been a sharp frost, which makes for better walking, and stiffens things up, in more ways than one. The soft fruits, and vibrantly coloured vegetables of summer seem a long, long, way away. They have all been replaced by the winter team of beetroot the colour of rich Pinot Noir, dark and inky red cabbage, brassicas, curly kale, and cavolo nero. These veggies seem the perfect partner to our abundance of game, soaking up all of the rich, tasty juices.

The appearance of buttered Brussels sprouts now points towards the festive season and the arrival of the annual Nativity Play. This year it is starring a certain Louis Pern, clad in mini-chef's jacket and a black Star Inn apron. He's cast, of course, as the Innkeeper!! He's a natural... Unfortunately, there was still no room at the inn, even in the kingdom of Pernshire.

On the shortest day, the sun is a deep, blood red and orange colour, like that of a Christmas clementine. It looks like a giant ball of fire on the horizon, or a pot of molten lava pouring slowly down as it melts over the Moors.

Shooting

Woodcock, or Timberwillies as they
are known on a certain local shoot
very near Rievaulx Abbey, are
regarded as the finest tasting of all
game. It's a small bird, which flits,
zig-zagging along, evading the gun
and its pellets. It can be eaten
whole, guts and all, as it defecates
on take-off and its entrails turn
almost to liquid when it is cooked.

Woodcock seem to appear
very rarely and are expensive
to purchase, no doubt due to
their scarcity in the market.
They are said to come in from
the Continent, heading to a
slightly warmer climate.
Many guns don't like to shoot
them, others find them an
impossible target to resist,
but the 'Bag' will never reach
double figures on a normal day.

'The flesh of the woodcock is
still held in high estimation!', as
Mrs Beeton put it. The woodcock's
junior counterpart, the snipe,
is reported to be the favourite
breakfast of a certain ex-Prime
Minister of our noble land, Sir
Winston Churchill. He would
eat a couple, simply roasted and
placed on toast together with a
bottle of Pol Roger champagne
to help wash it down!
No wonder we won the war!

Mixed Bag

**'SALADE PÉRNIGOURDINE':
QUAIL, FRIED QUAIL
EGGS, LARDONS, TRUFFLE
SHAVINGS, FRISSÉE
ENDIVE, CROÛTONS,
WILD MUSHROOMS AND
SHERRY VINAIGRETTE**

282_285

**POT-ROAST WOODCOCK
WITH SCRAMBLED VILLAGE
HENS' EGG 'CARÊME' AND
TARRAGON JUICES**

286_289

**SALAD OF WHITBY
LOBSTER 'NIÇOISE'-
STYLE WITH 'MOLLET'
LEDSTONE QUAIL EGGS,
MARINADED ANCHOVIES
AND GARDEN BEANS**

290_293

**SNIPE ON SPELT TOAST
WITH YOADWATH MILL
AIR-DRIED HAM AND
AMPLEFORTH ABBEY
APPLE BRANDY JUICES**

294_297

**GULLS' EGG WITH SAND
HUTTON ASPARAGUS,
ANCHOVY MAYONNAISE
AND FENNEL SHOOTS**

Wine Notes -
Woodcock & Lobster
by Andrew Firth

Woodcock is one of the best game
birds, a great testing shot and,
even though it does not have much
meat, it is very tasty and satisfying
with strong, quirky flavours, and
deserves a similar choice of wine.
I would go for a quality Valpolicella
Ripasso or, perhaps, a Cahors,
something from California, like a
Petit Syrah, or a Carmenere from
Chile. It's hard to serve white wine,
but, maybe a Gewurztraminer
would hang on in there, and put up
a good fight with the other flavours!

Lobster needs Champagne, as it's
always a treat and so is Champagne.
If you are too 'bah humbug' for that,
then it's back to Chardonnay.

At another legendary party at our 14th century, low-beamed thatched inn, the 'Rolling Stones' were live, for one night only. It was a night to remember and practically raised the roof, featuring Elliot, the Scotsman from sunny Stranraer, as Mick Jagger. With the Guinness pump as his microphone, he definitely had no 'sympathy for the Devil', and, unfortunately, 'couldn't get any satisfaction' either! As he thumped on the cellar door with his right foot for his bass drum, yours truly was playing a mean copper beer tray and providing, apparently astonishing, backing vocals. Meanwhile, Billy Calvert (aka Charlie Watts), played the drums using wine bottles and beer pumps, and his Belgian business associate looked on in a strange, Keith Richards'-like trance – another epic evening, etched into Harome folklore, that we still talk about to this day.

We've had our fair share of nights like that, which are always very much spur-of-the-moment, never organised or planned, but always memorable. People always say to me 'why didn't you tell me?', or, 'why didn't you let me know?', but I never know myself until after the event!

The local Harome Shoot dine with us several times a season. They're a mixed bunch, even a motley crew in one or two cases, but all are great fun. They're a cross-section of our community, made up of businessmen, builders, farmers, architects, and the like. The social event of their year is the Christmas party, when the 'wags' join the boys in the bar in late afternoon. There is usually a fairly substantial cheeseboard of Stilton, Wensleydale, fruit cake and Parkin provided to soak up the ale.

In the evening, hymn sheets come out, and 'Hark the Herald Angels Sing!' and various other renditions of festive favourites can be heard throughout the village. Ian Otterburn, our choirmaster, Nick Marwood, Chas Pickard and John Thompson all sing with gusto. Not the angelic sounds you would normally associate with the serenity of a Christmas carol service – 'Peace on Earth', it certainly ain't! As the night goes on, competitive spirit usually comes to the fore, with talk fuelled by seasonal merriment and ale. We've had late-night golf demonstrations using a makeshift nine iron (an old shepherd's crook, lifted down from the beams), and an orange for a golf ball. The golfer teed off with a wiggle of his hips, and a swipe, and then a huge swing at the citrus ball which flew directly into the mirror over the fireplace – at that moment, you know home time beckons.

The shoots that take place closer to the Christmas period are always 'up for a party'. We are never short of a reason to let our hair down. The guns who 'shoot through' tend to arrive early at the Wheelhouse, after trudging through the Moors and woodland, building up their appetite as they go. After a big late lunch, they generally retire to the pub for a little more physical exertion. This time, it's in the form of a marathon game of dominoes, with intermittent fag breaks, or a game of cards, where a single 'hand' can cost them the price of a day's shooting.

With all of these feats of endurance taking place and booze flowing at a steady old pace, 'our guns' start getting peckish, so snacks are 'drip-fed' to them throughout late afternoon and into the evening. On one particular memorable night, there was a shooting party with us, all the way from West Yorkshire, who had already attacked various bottles of very expensive wine throughout the evening. As often happens in the early hours, the munchies set in, and a request came through from our hotel, "Can we call for a takeaway?". Slightly bemused, we asked what they meant. "Curry!", was their reply.

Curry, in Harome??!? At 1am!!?! "No chance", wasn't actually the reply they got, but it probably came across that way, judging by expressions on the faces of our locals. So, as ever, stepping in with both feet first, "I'll make one!", sprang from my lips, before my brain had chance to engage. With several ales on board, I set off on a mission to prepare a Ryedale Rogan Josh (or, at least attempt to). One diced whole beef fillet, various spices, mango, tomato, and even coconut milk, simmered for approximately 15 minutes, and there I had it – a medium-rare 'Ruby Murray', with wild mushroom rice and even a raita for accompaniment. How's that for going the extra mile? It was, indeed, a veritable feast and is still talked about in the pub to this day – a legend in the Harome 'Hall of Fame'.

'SALADE PÉRNIGOURDINE': QUAIL, FRIED QUAIL EGGS, LARDONS, TRUFFLE SHAVINGS, FRISSÉE ENDIVE, CROÛTONS, WILD MUSHROOMS AND SHERRY VINAIGRETTE

Starter/Snack - Serves two
Preparation time: 40 minutes
Cooking time: 25 minutes

2 corn-fed quail, gutted
    and trussed
2 quail egg
8 slices black truffle
25g pancetta lardons
100g frissée endive
10g croutons, 1cm dice
50g seasonal wild mushrooms
a splash of white truffle oil
50ml veal jus
20g unsalted butter
a splash of olive oil
celery salt

for the sherry vinaigrette
100ml sherry vinegar
20ml rapeseed oil
1 tsp grain mustard
a sprinkle of sugar or
    a dot of honey
seasoning

to garnish
fresh herbs and edible flowers

In a little oil and 10g butter, colour the seasoned quail until golden brown, then place into a hot oven for 10 minutes. When cooked, remove and allow to rest. Whilst the quail are in the oven, fry the mushrooms and lardons in a little oil and cook the quail eggs in a little butter in a separate pan. To make the vinaigrette, place all of the ingredients into a bowl and whisk together, or place in a jar and shake it, shake it Baby! Dress the endive with the vinaigrette and add the croutons.

Place the salad onto a plate or bowl, carve the breasts and legs from the bird and arrange on the salad. Spoon the fried mushrooms and bacon over, with the quail eggs on top, and a few truffle shavings to finish. Garnish with fresh herbs and edible flowers. Serve immediately.

A LIGHT DISH WHICH I'VE SOMEWHAT ANGLICISED. IT WAS ON THE MENU AT MONTCOURT-FROMONVILLE AT L'HOSTELLERIE DES TROIS SOURCES, MY FIRST PLACE OF WORK ON FOREIGN SOIL, IN A BEAUTIFUL FAMILY-RUN HOTEL AND RESTAURANT BY THE LOING CANAL, NEAR FONTAINEBLEAU. AS THE DISH HAS TRAVELLED TO YORKSHIRE, THE 'FOOD CAPITAL OF EUROPE', IT HAS BECOME KNOWN BY CERTAIN LUMINARIES AS 'PÉRNIGOURDINE' RATHER THAN 'PÉRIGOURDINE' [THE FAMOUS TERM FOR DISHES INCORPORATING TRUFFLE]…. WELL, BECAUSE IT'S MINE REALLY, NO OTHER REASON!

POT-ROAST WOODCOCK WITH SCRAMBLED VILLAGE HENS' EGG 'CARÊME' AND TARRAGON JUICES

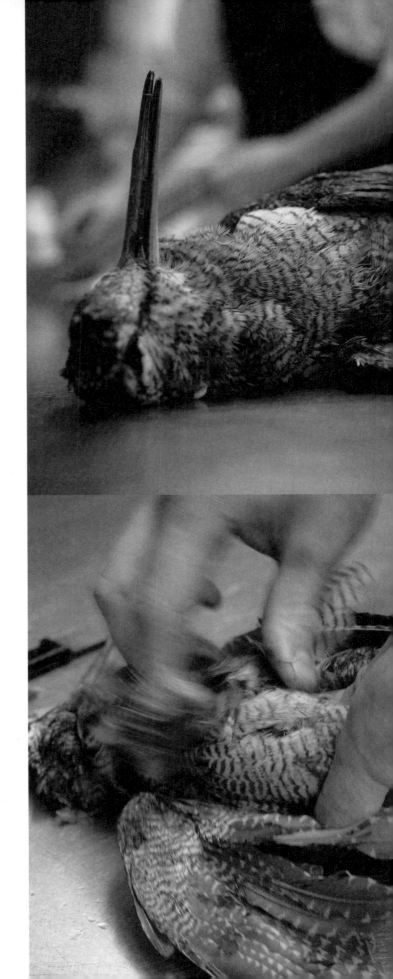

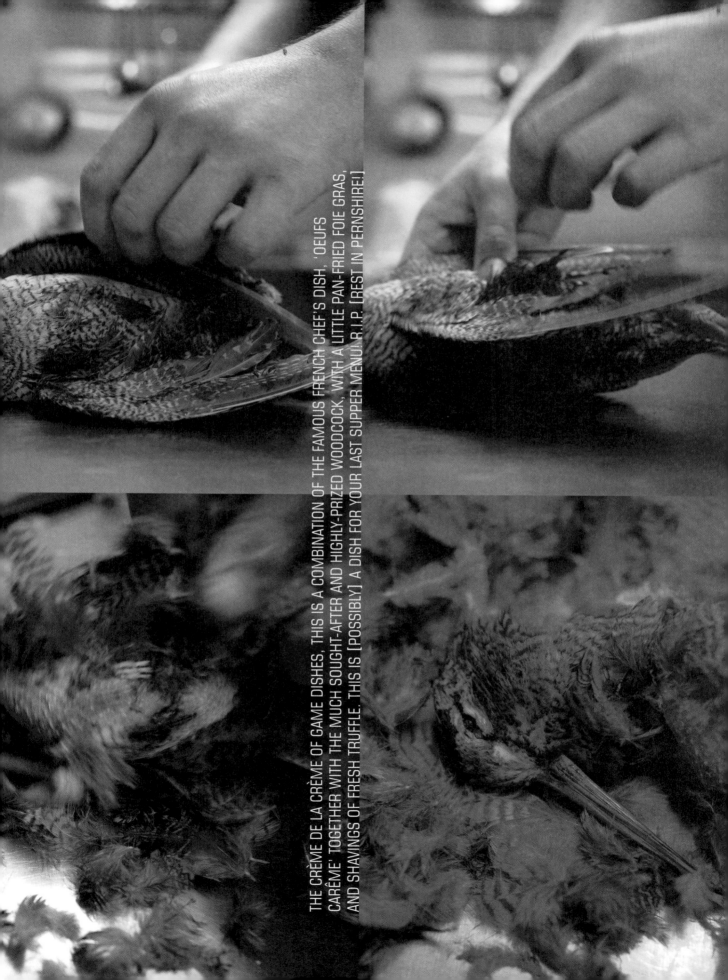

THE CRÈME DE LA CRÈME OF GAME DISHES, THIS IS A COMBINATION OF THE FAMOUS FRENCH CHEF'S DISH, 'OEUFS CARÊME' TOGETHER WITH THE MUCH SOUGHT-AFTER AND HIGHLY-PRIZED WOODCOCK, WITH A LITTLE PAN-FRIED FOIE GRAS, AND SHAVINGS OF FRESH TRUFFLE. THIS IS [POSSIBLY] A DISH FOR YOUR LAST SUPPER MENU! R.I.P. [REST IN PERNSHIRE!]

POT-ROAST WOODCOCK WITH SCRAMBLED VILLAGE HENS' EGG 'CARÊME' AND TARRAGON JUICES

Main course - Serves one
Preparation time: 20 minutes
Cooking time: 30 minutes

1 woodcock, dressed with head on [twist the head around the side of the body pushing its beak through the thigh to 'truss' the bird].
a little softened butter
1 egg
30ml cream
a knob of unsalted butter
½ slice of foie gras, seasoned
1 measure of Madeira wine
50ml veal jus
a few tarragon leaves
a few shavings of winter truffle
a splash of truffle oil

284_285

Preheat the oven to fairly hot 220°C/gas mark 7.

Lightly brush or coat the woodcock with softened butter. Season. Place into the oven for 12 minutes. When the bird is cooked, remove from the oven. Keep warm and allow to rest on a separate tray. Split the head longways, arrange onto a warmed plate. Remove the breasts and legs, and arrange these onto the same plate. Keep warm.

Crack the egg into a little pan with the cream and a knob of butter, whisk thoroughly and cook gently over a low heat (using a wooden spoon so as not to discolour). When nearly cooked, remove from the heat, then in a hot pan, pan fry the seasoned foie gras with no oil or butter for one minute each side, remove and drain on kitchen paper.

Warm the Madeira and veal juices, reducing to a syrupy consistency and drop in the tarragon leaves at the last minute. Pour into a sauce boat and serve separately.

To serve, place the foie gras onto the plate with the woodcock arranged around it. Check the seasoning and consistency of the egg and spoon onto the plate or place in a suitable vessel. Drizzle over the truffle oil and garnish with a few truffle shavings. Serve immediately.

SALAD OF
WHITBY LOBSTER
'NIÇOISE'-STYLE
WITH 'MOLLET'
LEDSTONE
QUAIL EGGS,
MARINADED
ANCHOVIES AND
GARDEN BEANS

THIS IS A FRESH, ZINGY SALAD, WHICH HAS REALLY
GOT INTO THE BOOK BY A FLUKE, BUT THE NIÇOISE SALAD
WOULDN'T BE ANYWHERE NEAR AS GOOD WITHOUT THE EGGS.
HERE, WE HAVE USED QUAIL EGGS, BUT PHEASANT EGGS ARE
ALSO BEAUTIFUL, AS ARE DUCK EGGS — AND WOULD BE A
MORE SUBSTANTIAL MAIN COURSE. WHATEVER YOU DECIDE,
IT'S BLOODY LOVELY!

Clean and prepare the lobster, remove the tail meat and slice into 5 or so thin slices, crush the claw meat and set aside.

Cook the quail eggs and green beans in separate pans of salted, boiling water for 2 minutes and 1 minute respectively, then refresh both in iced, or at least very cold, water. Drain well and mix the green beans with the black olives, tomatoes and potatoes, season with sea salt and drizzle with olive oil. Remove the shells from the quails' eggs and cut in half.

To serve, place half of the salad onto each plate (or into a nifty mini colander, like we do), with the lobster on top. Garnish with the anchovies, garden herbs and quails' eggs. Then put on your sunglasses and pretend that you're dining on the Côte d'Azur!!

Starter - Serves two
Preparation time: 20 minutes
Cooking time: 10 minutes

1 x 450-500g native lobster, cooked
    for 10 minutes, split and dressed
6 quails' eggs
100g green beans, topped
    and tailed
50g black olives
50g new potatoes, peeled,
    cooked and diced
a pinch of sea salt
10ml olive oil
6 cherry tomatoes,halved

to garnish
80g marinated anchovies
mixed garden salad, leaves
    and edible flowers

**SALAD OF WHITBY LOBSTER
'NIÇOISE'-STYLE WITH
'MOLLET' LEDSTONE QUAIL
EGGS, MARINADED ANCHOVIES
AND GARDEN BEANS**

SNIPE ON SPELT TOAST WITH YOADWATH MILL AIR-DRIED HAM AND AMPLEFORTH ABBEY APPLE BRANDY JUICES

THE LITTLE SKINNY SNIPE NEEDS A HELPING HAND [OR WING] SO WE'VE BUILT HIM UP WITH SOME SUCCULENT AIR-DRIED HAM, A THICK SLICE OF BREAD AND SET HIM ON HIS WAY WITH A NIP OF AMPLEFORTH APPLE BRANDY.

Preheat the oven to 200°C/ gas mark 6.

Take the dressed snipe, but do not gut. Remove the wings and the lower leg sections (crack the bone, twist and pull to remove the sinews). Season the birds and wrap with the air-dried ham. Colour in a little butter and oil, then place in the hot oven for 4 to 5 minutes. Remove from the oven, but keep warm.

Shallow-fry the spelt bread in the dripping. Keep warm. Deglaze the roasting tray with the apple brandy and add a little chilled butter.

Remove the breasts and legs from the birds, chop the ham and arrange on the fried bread, brush with melted butter and season. Pour the apple brandy and juices over and serve immediately.

Starter/Snack - Serves two
Preparation time: 20 minutes
Cooking time: 15 minutes

4 snipe, dressed but with innards
4 slices of spelt bread
4 slices of Yoadwith Mill
   air-dried ham
50g butter plus 50g chilled butter
50g dripping
2 measures Ampleforth Abbey
   apple brandy, or similar
a little rapeseed oil
seasoning

292_293

SNIPE ON SPELT TOAST WITH YOADWATH MILL AIR-DRIED HAM AND AMPLEFORTH ABBEY APPLE BRANDY JUICES

GULLS' EGG WITH SAND HUTTON ASPARAGUS, ANCHOVY MAYONNAISE AND FENNEL SHOOTS

THESE BEAUTIFUL-LOOKING EGGS HAVE A BIT OF A STORY TO THEM, COMPARED WITH YOUR AVERAGE EGG. THE BLUISH-TINGED SHELL SURROUNDS THE DEEP YELLOW YOLK WITH ONLY A THIN LAYER OF WHITE. THE EGGS ARE SLIGHTLY POINTED ENSURING THEY DON'T ROLL OUT OF THEIR NESTS, WHICH ALMOST SEEM TO CLING TO THE CLIFF SIDES.

294_295

LESSER BLACK-BACKED GULL
- *Larus fuscus* -

BLACK-HEADED GULL
- *Larus ridibundus* -

COMMON GULL
- *Larus Canus* -

GREAT BLACK-BACKED GULL
- Larus marinus -

GREAT SKUA
- Stercorarius skua -

ARCTIC SKUA
- Stercorarius parasiticus -

HERRING GULL
- Larus argentatus -

KITTIWAKE
- Rissa tridactyla -

GULLS' EGG WITH SAND HUTTON ASPARAGUS, ANCHOVY MAYONNAISE AND FENNEL SHOOTS

Starter/Snack - Serves four
Preparation time: 10 minutes
Cooking time: 10 minutes

4 gull's eggs
16 asparagus spears
50g fennel shoots
a little melted butter
a little black pepper

for the mayonnaise
30g marinaded anchovies,
    finely chopped
2 hen egg yolks
1 tsp English mustard
50ml Wharfe Valley rapeseed oil
lemon juice from 1/2 lemon
salt and white pepper

to garnish
50g fennel shoots

First prepare the mayonnaise, by combining the egg yolks and mustard in a food processor, then gently drizzling in the oil. When emulsified, add the anchovies and lemon juice, then blitz for 30 seconds. Check seasoning and pour into 4 small pots.

Place the gulls' eggs into cold, salted water and bring to the boil. Simmer gently for 5$\frac{1}{2}$ minutes, then lift out and place onto a paper towel.

Whilst the eggs are cooking, drop the asparagus spears into boiling, salted water for 2 minutes. Remove, when cooked. Place on a paper towel and brush lightly with melted butter and season.

Gently 'saw' off the tops of the eggs and place into egg cups. Place each egg cup onto a plate with a pot of the mayonnaise, and 4 asparagus spears. Sprinkle a little black pepper onto the egg and arrange a few fennel shoots around the plate. Serve immediately.

GUILLEMOT AND RAZOR-BILL EGGS WERE MAINLY COLLECTED ALONG THE NORTH SEA COAST: MY UNCLE COLIN'S FARM, 'WIDDYFIELDS', PERCHED ON THE EDGE OF THE CLIFFS AT HAWSKER, JUST SOUTH OF WHITBY, WAS A PERFECT LOCATION FOR THEM. IN THE OLD DAYS, A 'PICKER' WOULD BE DANGLED SPIDERMAN-STYLE OVER THE CLIFF, WITH THREE OR FOUR MEN HOLDING ONTO THE END OF THE ROPE, LIKE ONE HALF OF A TUG-O-WAR TEAM. THE PICKER'S ONLY PROTECTION FROM PECKING BEAKS AND LOOSE ROCKS WOULD BE A BOWLER HAT FILLED WITH NEWSPAPER AND STRAW!

TIPPLES

NIBBLES 'N

Who would ever dream of having a day's shooting without a little sustenance to keep you going, and to absorb a little alcohol? As with the 'Hip Flask', everyone has their particular favourite. One of our regulars, Tim Crowley, often brings his own rillette, baguettes, and cornichons acquired on day-trips to Boulogne, and swills them down with our own Game Tea, followed by a slice of Shooters' Game Pie. Perfect!

Bait Box

Wine Notes - Bait Box
by Andrew Firth

A few drinks that work well in
the field, and in the home, are
Sloegasm, a mixture of Sloe Gin
(homemade, of course) and fizz,
such as Cava or Prosecco, works
very well. Riesling, as an aperitif,
is fresh and fruity and low in
alcohol (only 10%!) or Damson Gin,
Raspberry Vodka, Bramble Whisky,
Whisky Mac, Royal Ginger Liqueur.

In September, summer's finally over. We're now on the long run-up to Christmas. Within days, the seasons shift and the light slips away. Swallows feed like maniacs in their hundreds, sweeping around the giant sycamore tree outside the pub, and then fly along the lane. They line up on the telephone wires, as if on the starting line, ready for their epic 4,000 mile migration to the warmth of the African sun. This marks the true end of summer, along with the loud 'bang' of the partridge shooters, and the smell of the year's final harvested straw-bales which lie dotted around the fields, waiting to be picked up.

Our yearly glut of autumn fruits and berries come at the perfect time to get ahead of the game. They're ideal for making chutneys and relishes which will partner the pies, terrines, and pasties which we make using produce provided by the local shoots.

The sun rolls out of bed at around 8.15am, as the shooting boys and beaters get started for the day. Each hour is vital to a good day's shooting. The warmer and colder climates begin to clash, causing fog to descend daily on Ryedale.

A full belly is needed for a day on and off the field. A good friend of my dad, the late Hugh Riddolls (who was a sort of pre-Oliver Reed character, with similar hell-raising tendencies) had fallen asleep one day in our lounge, after a long day's shoot and eating his fill. Nobody could wake him. I don't think he could hear us over the noise of his own snoring! My dad's bright idea for a wake-up call was to get his 12 bore, open the lounge window, and blast a couple of barrels above Hugh's head. Before we knew it, everybody had near-perforated eardrums, and a ringing sound in their ears for days. And, as for Mr Riddoll, he didn't even move, and remained in a deep sleep all night. Mind you, he was in a very comfortable and extremely hospitable place...

BAIT BOX: A LITTLE SUSTENANCE NEVER GOES AMISS! WHETHER YOUR FAVORITE IS A SIMPLE SLICE OF CUTTING PIE, SAUSAGE ROLLS, OR A PASTIE - THEY'RE ALL A PERFECT ACCOMPANIMENT TO A COLD WINTERS' DAY.

**HARD-BOILED PHEASANT EGGS
WITH LOVAGE MAYONNAISE**

A SIMPLE APPETISER OR
SNACK, THESE MEDIUM-
SIZED MOTTLED EGGS ARE
ABSOLUTELY PERFECT.
USE HALF A DOZEN OR SO,
WITH THE CELERY-SCENTED
LOVAGE MAYONNAISE AND,
MAYBE, A SPRINKLE OF
CELERY SALT – THAT'S ALL
IT NEEDS – LESS IS MORE!

HARD-BOILED PHEASANT EGGS WITH LOVAGE MAYONNAISE

Snack - Serves one
Preparation time: 5 minutes
Cooking time: 10 minutes

6 pheasant eggs
5g garden lovage
20g mayonnaise, homemade
    preferably, otherwise a good
    quality supermarket version
a sprinkling of celery salt

to garnish
celery cress

Drop the pheasant eggs into boiling water and boil for 5 minutes. Remove and refresh in ice cold water, then peel. Finely chop the garden lovage and mix with the mayonnaise. Place the eggs on to a plate. Finely slice off the bottoms, so they will stand up and place a dot of mayonnaise on top. Garnish with celery cress or any other herb of your preference. A sprinkling of celery salt is a nice finish.

306_307

GAME TEA WITH SAGE
AND ONION DUMPLINGS

Snack - Serves ten
Preparation time: 30 minutes
Cooking time: 4 hours

2kg game carcases
2 large onions, roughly chopped
6 carrots, roughly chopped
1 head celery, roughly chopped
2 leeks, roughly chopped
10 pink peppercorns
2 bay leaves
a little rapeseed oil
50ml sherry
50ml Madeira wine
5 ltrs water to cover

for the dumplings
30g suet, minced
a pinch of garden sage, chopped
70g plain flour
a little salt
5g cracked black pepper
10g onion, finely diced

Roast the game bones at 180°C/ gas mark 4 until golden brown. Heat the oil in a large pan, add all of the chopped vegetables and until beginning to colour. Deglaze the pan with the sherry and Madeira, then add the roasted bones and cover with water. Add the peppercorns and bayleaves, then simmer for 3 hours. Pass through a sieve lined with muslin, repeating as necessary to remove the solids. Season to taste and reheat as necessary.

To make the dumplings, combine all of the ingredients together and roll into 2cm balls. Poach in the game tea for 20 minutes.

308_309

A CONSOMMÉ REALLY, IN EVERYTHING BUT NAME, IT'S A DEEP MAHOGANY-COLOURED SOUP, FLAVOURED WITH MADEIRA AND SERVED PIPING HOT WITH THE LITTLE PEPPERY DUMPLINGS BOBBING AROUND IN IT. IMAGINE SITTING ON THE MOORS OVERLOOKING THE VASTNESS OF THE PURPLE HEATHER, THE WIND BLOWING AWAY THE COBWEBS, AND SIPPING SOME OF THIS CHARACTER-BUILDING 'SOUP' FROM A FLASK.

PHEASANT AND WALNUT PASTIE

Snack - Makes 10 pasties
Preparation time: 30 minutes
Cooking time: 30 minutes

for the pastry
[or use 1 packet of readymade
shortcrust or puff pastry,
if you wish!]
110g cold butter
170g plain flour
1 large egg yolk
a little sea salt
a splash of cold water
1 pinch mixed dried herbs

for the filling
500g pheasant breast and
    thigh meat, cut into 1cm dice
5g dried mixed herbs
5g crushed juniper
50g smoked bacon lardons,
    cut into 1cm strips
150g blanched vegetables,
    potato, carrot, swede,
    cut into 1cm dice
1 measure of port
50g walnut halves
200ml game stock
20g onion, finely diced
    and softened in a little oil
10g unsalted butter
5g cornflour
seasoning

for the eggwash
4 egg yolks
sprinkle of dried herbs,
    or poppy seeds

MEATY AND BURSTING WITH
FLAVOUR, THE PIECES OF
GAMEY PHEASANT WITH
DICED ROOT VEGETABLES AND
POTATO, THE CRUNCH OF THE
WALNUTS, ALL ENCASED IN
HERBY SHORTCRUST PASTRY
IS GREAT FOR A PICNIC OR
SERVED HOT WITH BUTTERY
MASH, PEPPERED SAVOY
CABBAGE AND A JUG OF
ONION GRAVY. IT ALSO MAKES
FANTASTIC BAIT FOR THE
DISCERNING FISH.

PHEASANT AND WALNUT PASTIE

To make the pastry, first cut the butter into small pieces. Sift the flour into a large bowl and rub in the butter until the texture is similar to small breadcrumbs. Add the egg yolk, herbs, salt and a splash of cold water, and combine together to form a stiff dough. Mix thoroughly, but don't 'overwork' it. Place in the fridge and allow to cool for around 30 minutes.

To make the filling

First place a little butter in a thick-bottomed pan, and fry off the pheasant, bacon, root vegetables and onion until golden brown. Add the walnuts, herbs and juniper, and stir thoroughly to colour, then add the port and stock. Bring to the boil, then simmer for approximately 5 minutes. Mix the cornflour with a little cold water and use this to thicken the sauce, check the seasoning, then leave to cool.

Preheat the oven at 200°C/ gas mark 6.

Remove the pastry from the fridge and roll out on a floured surface, to a thickness of a 50p piece, then cut into 15-20cm discs with a round cutter (or cut around a side plate). Glaze the rim of each disc with a little egg wash, then place a couple of dessertspoons of the cooled pheasant mix into the centre. Lift up the sides of the pastry discs to make a 'purse-like' pastie shape, then crimp the edge with your index finger and thumb to seal the pasty. Egg-wash all over the pasties and sprinkle them with a little more dried herbs and poppy seeds, then place on a lightly-greased baking tray and chill again for approximately 20 minutes to set. Place in the preheated oven for about 12 minutes, until crisp and golden brown. Allow to cool on a rack (for as long as you can resist!), or serve as a hearty lunch with mashed spuds, greens and gravy.

Starter - Makes 10 sausage rolls
Preparation time: 20 minutes
Cooking time: 10 minutes

for the pastry
[same as pheasant and walnut
pasties, again, you can substitute
500g good readymade quality puff
or shortcrust pastry, if you wish]
plus
2 egg yolks
a sprinkling of poppy seeds

for the filling
225g pork sausagemeat
225g mallard breast,
    skinless, finely diced
20gm of mixed peel
pinch of dried mixed herbs
50g white breadcrumbs
zest [fine] and juice of one
    large orange
a pinch of nutmeg
seasoning

for the eggwash
2 egg yolks
20g plain flour

Preheat the oven to 200°C/
gas mark 6.

First combine all of the filling
ingredients together and set
aside. Roll out the pastry to
a long strip approximately
30cm long, 15cm wide and the
thickness of a 50p piece and
arrange the mallard forcemeat
in a sausage-like fashion evenly
along the length of the strip
and seal the pastry around it.
Brush lightly with the eggwash
and sprinkle with poppy seeds.
Cook in the preheated oven for
approximately 10 minutes, until
the pastry is golden brown.
Remove from the oven and
place on a cooling tray, then
munch as required!

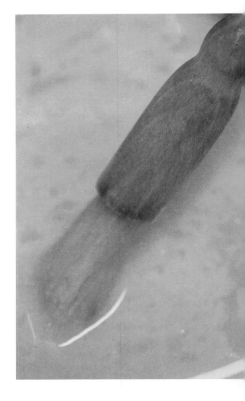

**MALLARD AND MIXED
PEEL SAUSAGE ROLL**

USING NORMAL BAKING MIXED PEEL, DRIED MIXED HERBS AND ORANGE ZEST, THE FINELY CHOPPED MALLARD BREAST IS BOUND WITH A LITTLE PORK SHOULDER SAUSAGEMEAT, THEN WRAPPED IN FULL BUTTER PUFF PASTRY, AND BAKED UNTIL GOLDEN BROWN. BEST EATEN WITHIN A FEW MINUTES OF COMING OUT OF THE OVEN.

SHOOTERS' GAME PIE

Snack - Serves twelve
Preparation time: 1 hour
Cooking time: 1½ hours
plus overnight chilling

500g hot water pastry
[see 'Loose Birds' Chicken,
Hawes Wensleydale and
Hambleton Ale Pie]
2 duck breasts
2 pheasant breasts
4 wood pigeon breasts
200g pork shoulder, minced
2 guinea fowl breasts
8 juniper berries
50g redcurrant jelly
4 tbsp sloe gin
2 gelatine leaves
100ml game stock
1 egg yolk [to glaze]
seasoning

Preheat the oven to 160°C/
gas mark 2-3.

First line a 20cm pie case with
the pastry and cut out a disc
of pastry for the lid. Cut all of
the game breasts into strips
longways approximately 5mm
thick. Season the pork and the
game meats. Now layer the pork
and breast meats inside the pie
case, repeating until all the meats
have been used. Brush the rim of
the pastry with the egg yolk, cut
a small hole in the centre of the
pastry lid (through which the jelly
will be poured when the pie is
cooked), then seal to the base.

Eggwash the lid and cook the pie
in the preheated oven for 1 hour.
Towards the end of the cooking
time for the pie, soak the leaf
gelatine in a little cold water, until
soft. Then bring the game stock,
sloe gin and redcurrant jelly to
the boil in a small saucepan, then
remove the pan from the heat
and add the soaked gelatine,
whisking until this is dissolved.
Add the juniper berries and allow
to cool a little without setting.

After the pie has been removed
from the oven, use a funnel to
pour the sweet jelly through
the hole in the lid, into the pie.
Allow to cool, then refrigerate
overnight. The jelly will set in a
similar way to that in a traditional
pork pie. Enjoy at will!

SHOOTERS' GAME PIE

A CUTTING PIE MADE DURING THE AUTUMN AND WINTER MONTHS. LAYERS OF LOCAL GAME ENHANCED WITH SLOE GIN AND A REDCURRANT JELLY, AND 'STUCK TOGETHER' WITH A PEPPERY, HERBED FORCEMEAT. GREAT WITH A CHUNK OF WENSLEYDALE CHEESE AND MAYBE THE ODD PICKLED ONION.

Our farmhouse was a long building with large rooms. We had a big kitchen, with whole hams hanging from the ceiling, and a large yellow bin with a black lid, full of fermenting home-brew. Storage heaters battled valiantly to heat the thick-walled old building. The double glazing on the bedroom windows comprised glass on the outside, and ice on the inside! All part of the character-building regime – just put another jumper on!

We had a big, open fireplace which smoked constantly. It was the type you could hide inside as a child, preferably when the fire wasn't lit. Having said that, if the fire was on, it would have been a really impressive hiding place!

The various tipples taken on, and off, a day's shoot vary, depending on each individual's taste. Everybody has his, or her, favourite, and you'll find each beverage normally has a story or tale to go with it. Whichever is taken, they all have one thing in common – to warm the soul in more ways than one! Cheers, good hunting!

On a visit to Germany with one of my schoolmates, Chris Lloyd, whose father was stationed out there in the Army, I decided to buy a souvenir Rumtopf. A Rumtopf is an earthenware vessel into which fruits are placed, layer upon layer, as they come into season. Each layer is topped up with rum, lightly covering the fruit. The end result is a deliciously fruity liqueur of juicy seasonal berries which can be used in decadent desserts, and the 'juices' can be used to warm the cockles on a cold day's shooting, or, in front of a sizzling log fire on a winter's night. I had decided to give it as a surprise Christmas present to my parents. I brought it back with me in July, so it was quite a challenge adding sun-kissed strawberries, raspberries and blackberries, and topping it up with autumn sloes and damsons.

However, my hiding place was at the back of my wardrobe. It took some explaining, five or six months down the line, as to why the bedroom of a fourteen year old boy smelt like a distillery. Mum and Dad still talk about it now, so I think it was worth all that effort, and it was definitely something that was not available 'off the shelf'.

I also remember times when my brother and I used to come back from school in winter to our old farmhouse. Dad would be out on a day's shooting, covering the woods, the hedgerows, and the semi-frozen ruts of the ploughed fields. You could tell when they were getting closer to home as the odd pitter-patter of lead-shot tapping on the kitchen windows got louder and louder. It started sounding like hailstones when they were nearly home, so we knew it was time to get the kettle on, and prepare for clouds of cigar smoke and the whiff of whisky to enter the house.

THE BAR.8.35AM
The meeting place for an early morning call, and a quick 'livener', before a day's shoot, out in the cold.

Hip Flask

One way or another, our family has always been involved with booze. Social events used to involve Grandpop's pink gins and his infamous gallons of home-brew, of which I seemed to be the only connoisseur (or was that victim?). I was possibly the only one stupid enough to sample its unique, 'subtle', yeasty taste. That might explain why I have never drunk bitter since...

PⓇOšT!*;-

BULLSHOT

A POWERFUL DROP, WHICH
IS GUARANTEED TO PUT
HAIRS ON YOUR CHEST –
LADIES BEWARE!
A CONCOCTION OF BEEF
CONSOMMÉ AND VODKA;
A CURE FOR A DECENT
HANGOVER. YOU START
TO FEEL BETTER WITH
EVERY SIP...

328_329

BULLSHOT

Warmer - Serves a crowd
Preparation time: 30 minutes
Cooking time: 4½ hours

4 parts consommé [see below]
1 part vodka of your choice
    [natural flavour]

for the consommé
2kg lean beef
1.5kg shin of beef [with bone,
    broken down into chunks by
    your butcher to maximise
    the flavour!]
sea salt
3 or 4 large carrots, roughly
    chopped
400g turnips, roughly chopped
100g parsnips, roughly chopped
350g leeks
2 sticks of celery, roughly sliced
1 medium-sized onion stuck
    with cloves
1 clove of garlic
1 sprig of thyme
½ bay leaf

Cut up the beef and put it all
into a big stockpot. Add 7 litres
of cold water. Bring to the boil
and carefully remove the scum
that forms on the surface.
Season with coarse salt (it is
better to adjust seasoning at
the end than to add too much
at the beginning!). Add the
carrots, turnips, parsnips, leeks
tied in a bundle, celery sticks,
onion, garlic, thyme and bay
leaf. Simmer very slowly, so that
boiling is hardly perceptible, for
4 hours. Remove the meat and
very carefully strain the stock.
Remove the surplus fat carefully.
Pass through a fine sieve or
muslin cloth. Use as required.

To serve, reheat and add the
vodka just before serving.

SPICED CITRUS WHISKY

THIS RECIPE WAS DONATED
BY KATE FENTON, VIA HER
MUM. KATE WAS THE
PARTNER OF THE LATE IAN
CARMICHAEL, THE FAMOUS
ACTOR OF JEEVES AND
WOOSTER FAME, WHO I HAVE
BASICALLY KNOWN ALL OF MY
LIFE, AS HE LIVED NEAR TO MY
PARENTS. HE WAS A LOVELY,
SLIGHTLY ECCENTRIC 'PROPER'
CHAP. THANK YOU FOR YOUR
HELP, KATE — WE'LL RAISE
A GLASS TO THE BOTH OF
YOU. CHEERS!

SPICED CITRUS WHISKY

Snifter - Serves: depends on who your friends are!
Preparation time: 20 minutes
Waiting time: a couple of months

4 oranges
200g sugar
2 tsp coriander seeds
1 litre whisky

Thinly peel the rind from the oranges, cut into thin strips and place in a jar or bottle. Squeeze out the juice and add to the jar, with the sugar and coriander seeds. Pour over the whisky and seal, then shake the bottle to start to dissolve the sugar. Leave in a cool, dark place for a couple of months, occasionally shaking the bottle, then strain and re-bottle.

THIS WHISKY GOES DOWN A STORM IN THE BEATERS' WAGON. THE ODD THING IS THAT YOU DON'T TASTE THE WHISKY, AS WHISKY, AT ALL, AS THE ORANGE AND SPICES COMPLETELY DOMINATE THE TASTE, SO THE SUPERMARKET'S CHEAPEST MCTARTAN DRAIN-CLEANER BRAND WILL DO JUST FINE. HAVING SAID THAT, KATE TELLS ME SHE HAS TASTED A VERSION ONE ENTHUSIAST [A GUN, AS NO BEATER WOULD BE SO DAFT] MADE WITH GLENFIDDICH AND, APPARENTLY, IT DID RETAIN A SLIGHTLY SMOKY, MALTY UNDERTONE, SO CHOOSE FOR YOURSELF.

AUGUST AND EARLY
SEPTEMBER ARE THE BEST
TIMES FOR MAKING PLUM
WINE, BUT PLUMS FREEZE
WELL IF THEY ARE HALVED
AND STONED, AND THIS WAY,
YOU CAN MAKE IT AT A LATER
DATE WHEN YOU HAVE MORE
TIME. THANKS TO MY DAD
FOR THIS RECIPE.

PLUM WINE

Refresher - Serves quite a few
Preparation time: 1 hour
Waiting time: 6 months

1.5kg plums, halved and stoned
1.5kg sugar [reduce to 1kg
    for a drier wine]
4.5 litres of boiling water
15g yeast

Place the plums in a bucket
and pour over the boiling water.
Cover and leave for 5 days,
stirring the contents a couple
of times each day. On the sixth
day, strain the plums and pour
the liquid back into the bucket.
Stir in the sugar and stir until
dissolved, then sprinkle in the
yeast and cover the contents
with a thick cloth. Stand the
bucket in a warm place, for
example a kitchen window for
three to six months or as long
as needs must. Strain the wine
a second time and tip all of the
wine into a demijohn, topping
up with water, if necessary.
Use a bored bung with a bubbler
airlock; the water in the airlock
should bubble regularly, showing
that the maturing process is
underway. The wine should
remain in the demijohn until
the bubbling stage has finished
and can then be bottled.

The result should be a lovely,
rich red, fruity wine drinkable
after 6 months.

WILD CHERRY CHOCOLATE BRANDY

338_339

JUST FOR A CHANGE,
DEPENDING ON WHICH
TREES ARE DOING WELL, IT'S
WORTH EXPERIMENTING WITH
DIFFERENT COMBINATIONS.
CHERRY BRANDY IS GOOD
WHEN THE FRUIT IS TOO
SMALL OR TOO TART TO BE
USED FOR MUCH ELSE.
THE STONES GIVE IT A
POWERFUL ALMOND-LIKE
PUNCH, WHICH IS JUST
THE THING ON A FROSTY
'PHEASANT' MORNING.

WILD CHERRY CHOCOLATE BRANDY

Comforter - Serves four/six
Preparation time: 10 minutes
Cooking time: 10 minutes

1 litre full cream whole milk
1 cinnamon stick
2 whole cloves
115g plain dark chocolate,
    chopped into small pieces
5 shots of wild cherry brandy
2-3 drops of almond essence

Bring the milk gently to the boil
with the spices added, remove
the spices, then turn the heat to
simmer and stir in the chocolate.
Continue stirring until melted,
add the brandy and almond
essence, then whizz on high
speed for about 30 seconds.
Pour into a pre-warmed flask.

340_341

THE HOT TODDY

The table boasts its being from Japan,
th'ingenious work of some great artisan.
China, where potters coarsest mould refine,
that rays through the transparent vessels shine;
the costly plates and dishes are from thence,
and Amazonia must her sweets dispence;
to her warm banks our vessels cut the main,
for the sweet product of her luscious cane.
Here Scotia does no costly tribute bring,
only some kettles full of todian spring.
Where Indus and the double Ganges flow,
on odorif'rous plains the leaves do grow,
chief of the treat, a plant the boast of fame,
sometimes call'd green, bohea's its greater name.
O happiest of herbs! who would not be
pythagoriz'd into the form of thee,
and with high transports act the part of tea?
Kisses on thee the haughty belles bestow,
while in thy steams their coral lips do glow;
thy vertues and thy flavour they commend,
while men, even beaux, with parched lips attend.

Extract form The Morning Interview by Allan Ramsay [1686 - 1758]

THE HOT TODDY

Medicinal - Serves one
Preparation time: 5 minutes
Cooking time: 5 minutes

a large measure of whisky
    of your choice
1 tsp good quality honey,
    such as Harome Honey
1 lump of brown sugar
slices of orange or lemon,
    whatever you prefer
50cl boiling water
a strip of fresh vanilla pod
    or cinnamon stick, according
    to personal preference

Mix together the whisky, honey,
a slice of lemon and a lump
of sugar, then top up with
boiling water, add the vanilla
or cinnamon to finish.

THE NAME TODDY MAY EITHER
HAVE COME FROM A SOURCE
OF WATER IN EDINBURGH,
WHICH WAS CALLED 'TOD'S
WELL', AS EXPLAINED BY ALLAN
RAMSAY, A FAMOUS SCOTTISH
POET BACK IN THE EARLY
1700'S, OR POSSIBLY IT CAME
FROM 'TORRIE', AN EARLY
17TH CENTURY WORD FOR
A DRINK, MADE FROM THE
SAP OF A PALM TREE IN THE
EAST INDIES. TAKE YOUR PICK!
PERFECT WHEN FEELING A
BIT WEARY AFTER A WET AND
COLD DAY ON THE MOOR!

CHEF'S PANTRY

TO GIVE MORE DEPTH OF
FLAVOUR, THESE CAN ALL BE
REDUCED DOWN FURTHER,
TO YOUR OWN PERSONAL
PREFERENCE. THE STOCKS
WILL ALL FREEZE WELL.

CHICKEN STOCK
/MAKES 10 LITRES

a good splash of olive oil,
    approximately 200ml
10 kg chicken carcasses,
drumsticks and/or winglets
1 bottle of decent white wine
2 leeks, washed and chopped
2 heads of celery, washed
    and chopped
a few black peppercorns, crushed
2-3 sprigs of thyme
2-3 bay leaves
15 litres water

Heat a little oil and place the
chicken bones into a thick-
bottomed roasting tray, lightly
colour and place into a hot
oven for 8 to 10 minutes to
cook through, but not colour.
Remove from oven, add the
white wine and deglaze the tray
removing all the sediment and
the goodness from the tray.

In another pan, add the remaining
oil, vegetables, herbs and
peppercorns, sweat but don't
colour, then add the bones and
top up with water. Bring to the
boil, skim and simmer for 2 to 3
hours. Pass through a fine sieve
again to remove the bones and
gunge, discard these, then in a
clean pan, reduce down your
stock to the required amount.
Use as needed.

FISH STOCK
/MAKES 10 LITRES

5kg white fish bones
2 onions, peeled and
    roughly chopped
1 lemon, cut in half
10 black peppercorns
a splash of olive oil
1 head of celery, washed
    and roughly chopped
2 leeks – white part only,
    thoroughly washed
15 litres water
5 bay leaves, fresh
1 x 75cl bottle dry white wine

Lightly sweat off the vegetables
in a little olive oil – do not colour.
Add the fish bones, peppercorns,
lemon, bay leaves and wine,
top up with water, bring to a
gently boil and skim off the
frothy impurities. Simmer for 20
minutes, reducing by a third.
Then remove from the heat
and allow to stand for 10 to 20
minutes to allow the sediment to
settle. Pass through a fine sieve
or chinois and use as required.

GAME STOCK
/MAKES 10 LITRES

a splash of olive oil
5kg game bones [pheasant,
    venison, partridge, etc]
5kg veal bones
½ calf's foot or a couple of
    pigs' trotters, both split
1 bottle decent red wine
10 juniper berries, crushed
2-3 sprigs of fresh thyme
2-3 bay leaves
1 head of celery, roughly chopped
5 large onions, roughly chopped
2 cloves fresh garlic,
    roughly chopped
20 litres water

Colour off the game and veal
bones gently in a little olive
oil, then place in a hot oven for
a further 30-40 minutes until
golden brown. When coloured,
drain the fat out of the tray and
put into a large stock/deep pan,
scrape any sediment from the
tray and pour into the pan with
the fat. Add the root vegetables
and herbs to the tray, colour until
golden brown, then add the red
wine again scraping any bits
from the bottom of the tray
and pour into the stock pan.
Cover with cold water and bring
to the boil, skim any impurities
off the top and simmer for 2 to
3 hours, continuing to skim as
necessary. When done, pass
through a fine-meshed sieve
or chinois into a clean pan,
reduce to required taste and
consistency. Use as required.

VEAL STOCK
/MAKES 10 LITRES

a splash of olive oil,
    approximately 200ml
10 kg veal knuckle bones
5 kg beef bones
½ calf's foot or a couple of
    pigs' trotters, both split
1 bottle decent red wine
5 large onions, roughly chopped
5 cloves of garlic, roughly chopped
2-3 sprigs of fresh thyme
2-3 bay leaves
1kg fresh tomato purée
20 litres water

With a bit of the olive oil, gently
colour the veal, beef and foot in
a thick-bottomed roasting tray.
When coloured, put into a hot
oven for a further 30-40 minutes
until golden brown, not burnt!
Then drain the fat out of the tray,
warm up the bones again in the
tray, scraping off the sediment,
which holds a lot of flavour. In a
separate deep pan, add the rest
of the oil, the onion, garlic and
herbs. Sweat until coloured and
lightly browned, add the tomato
purée. Then pour the bones with
the wine juices and sediment
into the same pan, top up with
water and bring to the boil.
Skim any frothy impurities off
the top, then reduce heat to a
simmer and watch it bubble for
3 to 4 hours, skimming at will.
Once you are happy with your
stock, sieve the bones and gunge
out using a fine-meshed sieve
or chinois. Next, at a medium to
hot heat, reduce down the stock
by two thirds, until it starts to go
slightly syrupy. It will then be
ready for use. If using at a later
date, once cooled the stock will
set and may have a layer of fat
on top, which can be easily
removed and discarded.

VEAL JUS
/MAKES 2 LITRES

10 litres veal stock
½ bottle Madeira wine
½ bottle cooking port
250g caster sugar

To make the veal stock into veal
jus, reduce down the stock by
half. Then, pour the Madeira and
port into a very hot pan, add the
sugar and reduce this down by
three quarters, add to the reduced
stock and reduce again by a half
to give a shiny, syrupy sauce with
a good depth of flavour.

HOUSE MAYONNAISE
/MAKES 2 PORTIONS

2 hen egg yolks
1 tsp English mustard
1 tsp white wine vinegar
50ml Wharfe Valley rapeseed oil
salt and white pepper

First, combine the egg yolks,
vinegar and mustard in a food
processor, then gently drizzle
in the oil continuing to blitz
until the mixture is thick.
When emulsified, check
seasoning. Use as required.

HOUSE VINAIGRETTE
/MAKES 2 PORTIONS

2 parts rapeseed oil
1 part white wine vinegar
1 part wholegrain mustard
seasoning

Whisk the vinegar and mustard
together until emulsified, gently
dribble the oil into it, whisking
all the time. Check seasoning,
if a little sharp a sprinkle of
caster sugar or a touch of runny
honey sometimes helps.
Use as required.

POSTSCRIPT
/STEVEN DOHERTY

I have known Andrew as a very close friend and colleague for over 10 years. I first learned of Andrew and the Star Inn's reputation when I was still cooking at the Punch Bowl Inn at Crosthwaite in Cumbria; the common factor being we were both featured in Diana Henry's acclaimed book 'The Gastro Pub Cook Book'. It was some years later before I managed to visit Harome. Everything I had heard and read was true. It is not often in our sometimes cold-hearted industry that reputations really do live up to expectations.

The Star has never disappointed on any level. The welcome is warm and genuine. The food is outstanding. The accommodation, quirky, eclectic but genuinely comforting. Amazing breakfasts. The hospitality in the pub, hearty and legendary.

Geographically, the Star Inn is perfectly placed for the game season and shooting in general. I've had a love affair with game since I was a child, watching Mum cooking rabbit and venison.

Then at Le Gavroche, from when the grouse arrived through to Christmas and the New Year, all of the 'Specials' would be game. We cooked everything from teal to snipe, hare and game tartes. People have come to realise how really good game is. Being organic/ wild and naturally low in cholesterol, it's perfect food. As Craig Stevenson of Braehead Foods says "When it's in the air, it's game; when it hits the ground, it's food".

However, it can be tricky to cook sometimes, so Andrew's superb new book highlights, shows and explains in great detail, how to get the best out of game with care and attention. Andrew's recipes will help you to get the best out of your game. The recipes, of course, all have the hallmark of Andrew's unique and gifted approach to handling and cooking such beautiful natural produce.

In general at The Star Inn, Andrew Pern's food is an extension of his character and personality; original, generous, very warm spirited, magnanimous in every sense but, above all, it's about love and passion. It's the way you feel when you eat Andrew's food; it's as if you've just fallen in love either for the first time or all over again, it just makes you glow inside. The Star Inn – still the best Gastro Pub in the country by far.

Steven Doherty acquired his eminent reputation working with some of the world's greatest chefs. He began his cookery career at the Savoy in London and then moved to Le Gavroche where he cooked alongside the legendary Albert and Michel Roux. He is now the Managing Director of The Cook School, Scotland.

INDEX

350_351

INDEX

Olive, or 'Chick' as she is known, is a must.
a) Because she wouldn't be in the book otherwise! and
b) She eats most things in sight and is a great advert for a chef's daughter....

ACKNOWLEDGEMENTS
/THANKS TO:

Anthony Hodgson, of course, who has yet again pulled it out of the bag with the look, the feel and the design of the whole book. The number of people who say they stroke me whilst they are lying in bed (the book cover that is!!) is quite extraordinary, to the point of disturbing. Anthony is brilliant to work alongside. Cheers, Mate! I think we've got another winner. Good Game! Good Game!

The photographer, Drew Gardner, for his relentless search for the perfect picture, be it in a running stream, or on the top of Chimney Bank with me pushing his car out of the snow when it's minus 18°C at 2pm in the afternoon, sun-baked moorland, or hot steaming kitchens. Whatever the topic, we always seem to manage to meet up for a pint at the end of the day's 'shooting'.

To all my suppliers, be they 'locals' or professionals. The quality of all the produce we use at The Star Inn makes my job a lot easier and even more enjoyable, when I can utilise nature's larder and let the seasons write our menus.

To Liane Stöckert from Schönwald for providing a fantastic selection of porcelain for our photography. To the chefs who have helped pluck, cook and serve some great game and poultry.

Andrew Burton's pies deserve a special mention, 'the food of the gods', and thanks also to Steve Smith for his sheer enthusiasm and hard work. Cheers, Lads! To Nicola Oldroyd for yet again managing to convert my worsening scrawl into a readable format, eventually.

Last, but by no means least, a special thank you to my family. I loved growing up with you, attempting to catch crayfish (maybe one day!), playing 'spot the first grouse' as we drove over the Moors, and being on Fez alert at all times! And finally to Frannie for looking after me and being my friend, when I needed someone special.

Without all of you and your continued support, this wouldn't have been possible. Thank you!

AFT

358_359

Hopefully, I've opened up, literally, a new chapter on the subject of Poultry, Game and 'Poisson', a lighter look at the traditionally dark autumnal and wintery foodstuff of game, the flaccid fishy business and the poor pale poultry affair of the foodstuffs which fill our day-to-day appetites. I believe I've offered a fresh look at presentation, and at combinations and contrasts.

The aim of the game is to hunt for the table, loose birds and wild game which are both wild in life and in taste, having roamed free of boundaries, eating what they choose.

The excitement comes from the 'thrill of the chase' in the magical surroundings of the bird or animal's chosen habitat, and also from the challenge of cooking a beast, which tends to taste of its diet, resulting in a whole individual experience each time you eat it. Every mouthful of 'meat' seems to be slightly different; every morsel brings a slightly new taste. It seems to me that the cooks and chefs that work with this food become free spirits themselves.

They are used to being in a confined space, disciplined and regimented in their ways, whilst cooking these provisions allows them space and the challenge to make good of the best nature has to offer, albeit for a limited season in some cases. This is what gets the adrenalin going, the heart racing, the juices flowing!

It has been a true pleasure writing this book as it has reminded me of how my life (and that of my family) has been surrounded by Loose Birds and Game, and what a major part it plays in my earliest, and some of my happiest, memories. It has always been a case of remembering the pictures in my mind, the problem was finding my way around the gallery! But I always knew they were in there somewhere!

Then, from this idyllic extreme to another... the long arduous hours in the kitchen which, strangely, still manage to give me immense enjoyment, happiness and fulfilment through my passion or, dare I say it, obsession with cooking.

ERWORD

/ANDREW PERN

AN OLD LECTURER OF MINE ONCE REMARKED, "YOU CAN TELL WHEN YOU'VE CRACKED IT WHEN YOU CAN'T TELL THE DIFFERENCE BETWEEN WORK AND PLEASURE". IF THAT'S THE CASE, I RECKON WE'VE GOT HER CRACKED. I HOPE YOU'VE ENJOYED THE RIDE AS MUCH AS I HAVE AND I HOPE THAT YOU HAVE HAD THE CHANCE TO TAKE IN SOME OF THE VARIED AND CAPTIVATING SCENERY ALONG THE WAY!

Until the next time... 'Game on!'

Loose Birds....

And Game !

When we think of a chef we see in our mind's eye a man who makes a living doing something he loves. He is a passionate soul, an artist. He works every hour on the clock (and some that aren't!) **BUT** when it comes to that rare moment when he can commit, be it all too briefly, to leisure then he goes out and plays and **PLAYS HARD!** What does chef do when surrounded by millions of God's own acres? He shoots for the pot of course! Pheasant, partridge, woodcock, snipe, rabbit, hare. A good shot, like chef, likes a really loose bird, a young, fit, beautiful specimen with firm tender flesh that flies high and fast. Once he has enough for the pot he comes in from the cold and warms his cockles truly satisfied with a day well spent with Loose Birds and Game!